27 JAN 2010

Cop On

Cop On

What it is and why *your* child needs it to survive and thrive in today's world

Colman Noctor

Gill & Macmillan

Gill & Macmillan
Hume Avenue, Park West, Dublin 12
www.gillmacmillanbooks.ie

© Colman Noctor 2015
978 07171 6654 1

Typography design by Make Communication
Print origination by O'K Graphic Design, Dublin
Printed and bound by CPI Group (UK) Ltd, CR0 4YY

This book is typeset in 11.5/16 pt Minion.

The paper used in this book comes from the wood pulp of
managed forests. For every tree felled, at least one tree is planted,
thereby renewing natural resources.

A CIP catalogue record for this book is available from the British
Library.

5 4 3 2

The Author

Colman Noctor is a child and adolescent psychotherapist with St Patrick's Mental Health Services. He specialises in the treatment of emotional disorders. As a self-confessed technology addict himself he has a keen interest in the effects of contemporary media on child development and mental health.

Colman is a frequent contributor to national media, including *The Irish Times*, *The Irish Independent* and Newstalk's 'Moncrief', 'Talking Point' and 'The Right Hook'. He was recently interviewed at Dublin's web summit where he discussed how the internet is changing our world and how we prepare our children for a future that we can't even imagine. He also contributed to the RTE documentary 'We Need to Talk About Porn'.

He lives in County Wicklow with his wife and three children.

I would like to thank my wife and three children for their support as I pursued my goal of writing this book, and also for allowing me to practise being a dad for the last number of years.

Thanks also to my parents and siblings, especially my inspirational sister, Eleanor, who has taught me the value of grit, resilience and cop on in the face of adversity.

Contents

SECTION TWO

TECHNOLOGY and FAMILY LIFE: bridging the generation gap and
leading by example

SECTION THREE
COP ON IN ACTION: maintaining good sense in real life

Introduction

WHAT TO EXPECT FROM THIS BOOK

I decided to write this book in response to the questions I get asked, many times over, by parents I meet through my clinical work as a child and adolescent psychotherapist. There are a few core questions that every parent has, and the answers are often hard to articulate in a concise way. The same questions crop up during various public talks and media panels to which I contribute.

Many books for parents look at how parents can respond to or manage difficult behaviours in their children, but few look at raising children in more general terms. This book hopes to outline ideas and strategies that can be used with *all* children, whether they exhibit behavioural issues or not.

It is true that you don't get a licence before you become a parent and that there is no definitive rule book that explains how to fulfil this complex and vital role. This book does not claim to be that panacea, but it does strive to describe how parents should take different approaches with different children. Many parents are perplexed as to how two of their children could have 'turned out' so differently. 'But we raised them exactly the same!' they say. This is the reason this book was not written in the 'five steps to being the perfect parent' format; I believe we need to raise our children in ways that reflect the natural features of *their* personalities. These elements include temperament, vulnerability and robustness – characteristics that vary from child to child.

In addition, it's important to remember that children and adolescents manage their struggles differently from adults. At the risk of being too simplistic, I think there are generally two types of young people, who can be broadly categorised as 'externalisers' and 'internalisers'. Externalising children and adolescents are normally openly demonstrative about their feelings, and they tend to present with behavioural expressions that are classed as 'difficult'. These children slam doors, swear, become agitated, dye their hair blue or get body piercings without permission. In short, they project their difficult feelings outwards. Internalisers, on the other hand, are more introspective with their difficulties. They tend to be objectively quiet, compliant children who do not present with behavioural problems. Rather, they tend to withdraw, isolate themselves and present as anxious, ruminating on whatever might be bothering them. Most mainstream parenting books and programmes tend to focus on helping parents manage the behaviours of externalising children, because they're more immediately obvious and problematical, but there are many ways that parents can help their internalising children too.

This book is for all parents of all types of children of all ages in all family settings. It sets out to try to answer the questions I am most frequently asked, the ones that are the most difficult to answer. With this book I aim to provide parents with an understanding of the 'whys' of their children's behaviour and in it I will try to explain why some children react differently from others when it comes to life's challenges. I will give parents some practical advice and help them to do what they can to safeguard their children.

I will address some of the particular challenges of being a parent today, notably the impact on children of the influence of technology and the media. I will also encourage parents to examine their own relationship with technology and its impact on family life, especially given the recent onslaught of digital and online technologies in our homes. Speaking to parents, I have learned that they feel a bit at sea when it comes to what to do about these recent advancements, and this is largely due to a disconnect between their world and their children's. Parents are often unsure as to how to negotiate this technological space with their child or teenager. Typically, their questions begin 'When should I' or 'What is the right time to', and my fairly uninspiring reply is usually along the lines of 'It all depends on the child.'

Over the course of this book I am going to describe, in the detail that these questions deserve, an outline of different parenting approaches for different types of child. Crucially, though, all the strategies I will discuss share an emphasis on developing the elements of personality that encourage robustness and cop on, skills that will serve all children well. I will also encourage parents to be aware of the contemporary challenges that young children and adolescents – and, by proxy, parents – face in modern-day Ireland.

─────

I have worked with children, teenagers and their families for the past 18 years, and I have seen up close the new challenges that parents face in raising children in Ireland today. I have worked with families through the Celtic Tiger, and I have met and treated the affectionately described 'Celtic Tiger Cubs' over the course of their development through their teenage years. I also now regularly work with families trying to adjust to quite significant post-Celtic Tiger financial and lifestyle adjustments, and I have become acutely aware of the effect this has on how they live their lives.

I have witnessed, and taken part in, the technological revolution. I can remember working in child and adolescent mental health services when the mobile phone was first becoming a feature of Irish society. As a consumer of technology myself, I have had to reflect on some of own my slip-ups and mistakes as I, like many of us these days, became hooked on technology. More importantly, I became a parent myself in recent years, which has given me new insight into the complexity of being an Irish parent trying to navigate these changing times.

Ultimately, this book's goal is to help parents become aware of core qualities that can sustain their children through the challenges they will inevitably face throughout their lives. Central to this is the need to foster resilience in children and how, as parents, we can protect our children's self-esteem and nurture their development by encouraging a sense of 'cop on'. In a time when traditional values are being challenged by whatever seems quicker and easier, I feel that some important building blocks of our personalities are being lost – a sense of cop on being the most basic one.

MY BACKGROUND

I am a child and adolescent psychotherapist and I have been working in this area for the last 15 years, both in Ireland and the UK. I began my career as a psychiatric nurse in Saint John of God Hospital in Stillorgan, Co. Dublin, in 1995. This was considered an unusual career choice for boys at the time. When I completed my Leaving Certificate, my decision to go into nursing was made on the basis that I did not want to go to university, and that I had been told that I was pretty unimpressive with my hands so a career as a tradesman was not a runner. To give you an idea of how young I was at the time, I remember thinking that a career in nursing promised a favourable girl-boy ratio on the job, which would surely improve my prospects of some romance. So my initial vocation for my new career was no more convincing than that. I was never the child who went around with a toy stethoscope around his neck, destined for a career in medicine, but just the opposite – a lost teenager, who accidentally ended up in psychiatry.

I recall this story every year at exam time when I'm invariably working with young people who are panicking about their career choices or who feel they aren't certain what they want to do after they leave school. As is often the case in such situations, it seems that everyone else you know has a plan and you're the only one with reservations. In telling my own story, I stress that no one knows what the future holds and I hope that this offers some form of reassurance – or at least a giggle at my expense. Even big decisions made on a whim can turn out for the best or turn out very well indeed, in my case.

I am extremely lucky as I now find myself in a career that I can honestly say I really love and continue, even after 18 years, to be completely passionate about. When I completed my psychiatric nurse training in 1998 in a class that comprised six men and six women – things had turned out differently from what I'd anticipated – I knew that I had made the right decision. My nurse training was of the old 'apprenticeship' model, which no longer exists, and it was very challenging. My parents were worried at the time about my career choice; they thought I wouldn't stick with it. Nurse training was demanding: it required me to head into a geriatric ward for a 13-hour shift on a Sunday morning, just as many of my peers who were in college were coming home from a night out. However, despite the less-than-favourable male-female ratio and the long hours, something kept me going to reach the finishing line.

Upon reflection, what kept me going was my passionate interest in the mental and psychological components of the human subject. There were many really difficult experiences during my training; I remember having to physically restrain acutely ill patients and witnessing disturbing procedures like electro-convulsive therapy. These were 'make or break' situations for a somewhat immature 18-year-old boy. However, after these events I found myself not traumatised or disturbed, but rather preoccupied with trying to understand the human behaviour that led to these experiences. My relentless pursuit of an understanding of the meaning behind behaviour was the catalyst for pursuing a career in psychoanalysis; I still question behaviour in my clinical work today.

My interest in working with children and adolescents began when I was on a clinical placement on Saint Anne's Adolescent Unit in Saint John of God Hospital. This was a turning point in my career, and my time there had a profound effect on directing my clinical interests. At Saint John of God's, I met young people who exhibited similar symptoms and difficulties to their older counterparts on the adult units but with one major difference: these symptoms and difficulties were only emerging. There was, I felt, a real window of opportunity to engage these young people and perhaps interrupt or re-route any negative patterns or behaviours. This is the motivation that attracts many professionals to this speciality, but it is one that can also lead to much disillusionment as it's very demanding work. I have found over the course of my career that many young people who seem to be at risk can, with the help of therapy and early intervention, instigate changes that lead them in a more positive direction. These are the cases that get me out of bed in the morning and keep me motivated to continue in this line of work.

Once I decided that I wanted to work with children and adolescents, I completed a postgraduate qualification in child and adolescent psychiatry in Dublin City University. Later, I moved to London, where I worked in the wonderful Great Ormond Street Hospital for a number of years. There I enjoyed many opportunities for further training, and I worked on some fascinatingly complex cases. I then moved to Edinburgh to work as nurse manager of the child and adolescent inpatient unit at the Royal Edinburgh Hospital until I returned to Ireland in 2003, when I joined the staff of Our Lady's Children's Hospital in Crumlin and the Lucena child and adolescent mental health services in south Dublin. It was soon after my return to Ireland that I began to develop a career in psychotherapy.

Psychotherapy was once described to me as 'the science of subjectivity', a definition that rings true for me. This definition suggests that everyone is entirely different and that multiple truths can co-exist in everyone's story. I am specifically interested in psychoanalysis, as it explores the conscious and unconscious motivations for our thoughts, feelings and behaviours. Psychoanalysis also examines the relevance of our earlier life experiences to our adult lives and attempts to link these events to our choices, desires and reactions. Psychoanalysis pays specific attention to early childhood experiences and attachment patterns, which I will refer to throughout the book. I completed a graduate diploma in psychoanalytic studies in Dublin Business School, and later a master's in child and adolescent psychoanalytic psychotherapy in Trinity College, Dublin. My time at Trinity offered me my first experience of working one on one with young people as a psychotherapist, which provided me with a perspective that guided me far beyond my professional work. I now understand my clinical work, myself and even my world through the existence and influence of the unconscious mind.

I have been working as a child and adolescent psychotherapist for the last nine years. My journey to here has taught me many things. I am privileged to be in contact with young people who are willing to describe to me the challenges of living in their world. Their stories are always complex and can be simultaneously harrowing and enlightening. The process of engaging young people in the psychotherapy process is always evolving, and so too are the skills required to be a psychotherapist. In working with children and adolescents, there is a fine line between being seen as trustworthy and coming across as just another authoritarian adult in their lives who knows best and tells them what to do. A core aspect of developing the therapy process is being honest, which I really do value and hold at the forefront of my approach. Experience has taught me that young people value honesty and appreciate it when someone trusts them with important information and doesn't try to hoodwink them. By setting out the parameters of the therapeutic relationship with my young clients in this way, I establish an expectation of honesty that I believe is the true measure of the process's success.

I have learned so much from speaking to young people about what they value in relationships and I try to implement what I have learned in how I go about what I do. I try very hard to listen to what is 'really' being asked for, which is often a real challenge. However, I believe it is always an investment of time well spent.

The young people I meet give me the inside track on developments within their culture as they happen, allowing me an insight into what it is like to grow up amid the current challenges of contemporary Ireland. Being in my mid-thirties means that I am far enough away from their world not to be threatening to it, yet near enough to it to understand some of the elements of it too. As one young person said to me, 'Colman, you are by no means cool, but you're not quite a dinosaur yet.' I took this as a compliment.

Over the course of this book, I will be borrowing from stories that young people have told me about what it's like to grow up in modern Ireland, and will try to pass some of this knowledge on to you. Unsurprisingly, when I told some of my young clients that I was about to write a book, they looked concerned, which I interpreted as 'Are you going to talk about me?' or 'Are you going to sell us out by telling parents our secrets?' I would like to reassure all my clients, past and present, that the contents of this book will be based on what are called 'composite clinical cases'. This means that any case examples will be a 'hybrid' collection of a number of young people's experiences, and I will not refer to any cases directly or in any identifiable way. Also, although I will give readers enough information to help them to assist their adolescent children if they are struggling, I am not going to supply them with ways to keep up surveillance on their children in such a way that they will never be able to do anything private again – that would be counter-productive. Everyone needs a few secrets and a good bit of privacy, especially in adolescence, so I have no issue in keeping some of that information out of the pages of this book.

What I do hope to outline are some of the changes that have occurred in Irish society over the past decade and to inform parents of the potential impact of these changes. I will suggest ways in which traditional parental and family values can be maintained in a society that seems committed to stamping them out. One of the main issues the book will focus on is the impact of technology on modern-day parenting. I have been left aghast on many occasions when young people of all ages tell me about the capacity of technologies that they use and are familiar with and the serious complications that can arise with their use. I am a self-confessed technology fan, and I regularly engage in the online world. I love technology, but I am becoming increasingly aware of the pitfalls of this relationship, and as a parent of three small children I feel obliged to become more aware of the evolution of technology in order to protect them on their inevitable journey through it.

As I will explain more comprehensively throughout the book, this is in no way a 'finger-wagging exercise' that criticises parents or their lax parenting in this technological age. I hope it will be the very opposite. In keeping with my policy of honesty and openness, I will refer to my own slips throughout the book, as I too have been lured by the technological seduction, and I will explain how I continually work to keep on top of it as I raise my own children.

Colman Noctor

- Child and Adolescent Psychoanalytical Psychotherapist and Registered Advanced Nurse Practitioner
- St Patrick's Adolescent Mental Health Services, Dublin

Section One

THE IRISH FAMILY TODAY: a return to cop on

WHO WE ARE: THE IRISH PARENTING EVOLUTION

We have been sold a bill of goods as Irish parents. We have been led to believe that raising children can be made to fit in with our many other goals in life, and that there should be a neat, easy path to doing it perfectly – we just have to find the right method, the right system, the right master plan, book, website or app and it will all come together. If we play Mozart to the baby in the womb, they will grow up to be more cultured and intelligent; if we follow this 'foolproof' method, our toddler will sleep through the night; we're encouraged to sign up our teenagers to endless hours of extracurricular activities, and we are told that all this can be done with relatively little effort, if we just get organised.

The truth of the matter is that raising children is difficult: fact. It always has been, and it always will be. It's a time-consuming part of life for which there is plenty of guidance available, but very little of it is useful in real life. There is an inevitable trial-and-error aspect of being a parent, and each child and their every life stage present different and equally difficult challenges. In short, being the 'perfect parent' is neither possible nor desirable, and the same goes for raising the 'perfect children'.

Being the 'perfect parent' is neither possible nor desirable, and the same goes for raising the 'perfect children'.

Irish parents today

Finding the simplest route to perfect family life has been

particularly appealing to Irish parents in recent years, and with good reason: we haven't had an easy run of it. The extreme changes we have experienced in contemporary Irish society over the last decade or so mean we have had to learn different ways of managing our families. The Celtic Tiger and post-Celtic Tiger periods have brought about new types of familial situations, the most common of which I'll deal with here.

I have coined some phrases to describe some of the new trends in family life, but only for purposes of clarity – the terms are not intended to denigrate any parent who identifies with the concepts described. In fact, some of these scenarios apply to me and my family. The situations described below are the direct result of contemporary societal changes and are by no means criticisms of how parents are raising their children. Indeed, I hope that you recognise some of your own family struggles here. In realising that you're not alone and that the way our society has changed has inevitably shaped the way we raise our children, I hope you feel empowered to identify some of modern parenthood's biggest shared challenges and make changes for the better to suit you and your family.

M50 Parents

Nowadays it is very common for both parents in a family to have to work full time. These parents most likely began their family during the Boom, and were sold the notion that everyone had to get on the property ladder or they would lose out royally in terms of their future. These parents are more than likely middle-income earners; during the property bubble, the areas they could best afford were quite far from where they worked, so they looked at houses in what would be generously described as the 'commuter belt'.

Under pressure to have a roof over their heads and promised that 'you will never lose on bricks and mortar', M50 Parents purchased their homes and as a result now have lengthy commutes to work. For many M50 Parents, this involves a commute of over an hour to and from work, and the majority of that time is spent in traffic.

So how does this style of life affect how these parents raise their children? M50 Parents have such long commutes to and from work that they have limited windows of time to spend with their children during the working week. A typical M50 Parent gets up at 6:30 or 7 a.m. to get their children ready to go to childcare, be it a local crèche or a child-minder. Their contact with their children in the morning, then, is limited to 30 to 45 minutes when everyone is tired, resentful of having to be up so early and under pressure – just ask any parent how many times they say, 'Hurry up!' on any given morning.

After this stressful window, M50 Parents drop their children to childcare and continue on to work through more traffic. After work is finished at 5 p.m. – if they're lucky – then comes the long commute home, via childcare. Typically, M50 Parents collect their children at around 6 or 6:30 p.m. Again, both parents and children are tired after a long day, and time pressure is a feature here too. M50 Parents get a minute-long 'handover' from the child-minder and continue the drive home. Once they're home, the evening mealtime and bedtime routines begin, depending on the age of the child. Once more, this is all done while watching the clock. This period of the evening is often described as the 'witching hour' by parents, as children are over-tired just before they

are due to go to bed and so are more prone to difficult
behaviour.

Over the course of a typical weekday, M50 Parents might
spend a total of an hour or two with their children, usually
conducted through a haze of exhaustion and perhaps
irritability – and that's just the parents. Having such limited
time with each other under such trying circumstances
undoubtedly has an impact on the relationship between
parent and child. But it also affects the other times that the
family gets to spend together under better, less stressful
circumstances – like at the weekends. Come Saturday, M50
Parents finally get a chance to spend some quality time with
their children. M50 Parents honestly and openly describe
'indulging' their children at the weekends specifically
because they 'only get this time to be together'. There are
many forces at work in this indulgence; many parents,
including myself, fall into this pattern due to a combination
of factors, including feelings of guilt, a sense of competition
with midweek caregivers, and a desire to compensate for
absence during the week.

As an M50 Parent myself, I understand: you don't want to
spend the little time you have with your children chastising
them or disciplining them for every little thing. As a result,
you pick your battles. Sometimes this level of tolerance can
be understood in the context of all the other days of the
week, but sometimes there's a temptation to simply spoil
your child. With my first child, I became acutely aware of
my own tendency towards this kind of behaviour, so I had to
ask myself what I was teaching my child by my indulgence.
If toleration of frustration, learning to wait, delaying
gratification and building inner resilience are what I want

my child to learn, then how does buying them gifts or giving into their every demand nurture those qualities? In short, it doesn't. So I have had to row back on this habit, which was hard luck for my second child.

For M50 Parents there can also be some conflicting expectations between their style of caregiving and that of their children's midweek caregiver. Often this causes confusion for their children, in addition to being difficult for the parents to manage. In many ways, M50 Parents feel obliged to the midweek caregiver; they often also fear that if they are overly demanding with their children's caregiver, or if they challenge their methods, the caregiver might take their frustration out on their children. The crèche horror stories revealed recently in the press spoke to every parent's fears about choosing who minds their children. So if a parent's problem with their child's caregiver isn't too big a problem, an M50 Parent frequently just 'grins and bears it'. This is an incredibly difficult thing to do for any parent, and, as we all know, biting your tongue is a tiresome and stressful activity.

Often, rather than taking advantage of parental guilt, children punish M50 Parents for their absence. One way for a child to do this is to demand to stay at childcare when being collected. This gut-wrenching experience is one I myself have undergone, and it makes for an effectively painful punishment. Another is for the child to refuse to engage with their parent on the drive home. I am sure many M50 Parents have asked their child, 'How did you get on today?' only to be met with a sulky turn to look out the window. These rejections are entirely normal reactions for small children, but they are nonetheless very painful for parents. The struggle for M50 Parents to try to create meaningful relationships with their children under such difficult circumstances is significant. In an ideal world, working part-time or a four-day week might help in managing these difficult dynamics, for one parent at least. But financial realities and the need to pay an enormous mortgage for that property miles out on the commuter belt (which now may be worth only a fraction of what M50 Parents continue to pay for it) mean that this is not always possible.

Striking the right balance can be difficult for all of us, but I believe it is not impossible. Much of this book will focus on getting the balance right in many different areas of parenting, and later I will suggest ways you can better use the time you do have with your children. I will outline the important interactions and sharing that build resilience in your child and in your relationship, and how you can improve the parent-child dynamic to avoid some of the pitfalls that are so typical of modern parenting. In the course of my work I have seen how some parents manage the M50 Parent role superbly well and I have borrowed many of their top tips. I will show you the importance of managing the expectations of both parents and children and how to create 'sacred spaces' for family interactions that are about time, not things.

Grandparent Parenting

In recent years there has been a move towards, or indeed back to, grandparents minding their grandchildren. In days of old, grandparents often played a central role in the family, and this trend seems to have re-emerged. In some cases, this is because parents can no longer afford crèches, au pairs or child-minders, so *their* parents (the children's grandparents) are asked to help out with child-minding duties during the week.

A wonderful consequence of this development is that children and their grandparents have been forming close relationships. This is indeed a very good thing and gives a great sense of comfort and validation to both parties. However, like M50 Parents, parents in a Grandparent Parenting situation can feel less involved with their children and indeed less like a primary caregiver. A child's close relationship with their grandparents can make parents worry about the quality of their own relationship with their child. It can also be quite difficult to manage the conflicting rules and expectations that grandparents set for their grandchildren compared with those of parents. It could be that Granny lets the child be cheeky, which she puts down to being 'spirited', or that Granddad sees no problem in giving the child four Jaffa Cakes on the drive home, just before dinner. Many parents feel that they can't say anything; after all, grandparents often provide childcare at a reduced rate of pay, if they are paid at all.

This dynamic is a difficult one to manage, as parents are incredibly grateful to their parents or their spouse's parents for minding their children, but it is not without its complications – complications that many parents are loath to admit exist. If your parents are now the primary caregivers for your children, this can also bring up its own trans-generational conflicts about how children should be raised. Unlike with child-minders from outside the family, parents in a Grandparent Parenting situation might worry that their children will experience problems with their grandparents that they know all too well from their own childhood. For example, one parent explained to me that her mother had always passed comments about people's weight, a quality that she really disliked. The woman's daughter was now making similarly disparaging comments about people's weight, which the woman was finding difficult to manage. She did not want to raise the issue with her own mother, because she felt obliged to say nothing, as her mother was minding her granddaughter as a favour.

A more serious concern is the impact on children of the loss of a grandparent through illness or bereavement, particularly if the grandparent is a primary caregiver to a child for a considerable period over their formative years. This can have a devastating effect on children, and can in many ways be experienced like losing a parent. Grandparent-grandchild relationships can be incredibly strong, and it is important to recognise that children experience grief with a similar intensity to adults, but perhaps before they are cognitively or emotionally ready to deal with it. Sometimes children are expected to adjust to this loss without adequate understanding or support and this can be problematic.

The involvement of grandparents in childcare can bring great benefits, including love, peace of mind and affordability. Yet like all family arrangements, it is not without its complications.

The GAA Tiger Mum

A prominent feature of contemporary Irish life for parents is what I call the 'GAA Tiger Mum'. The 'Tiger Mom' is a concept that originated in a book by Amy Chua in 2011 that described an aspect of Chua's experience of this stereotypical Chinese-American parenting style. The Tiger Mom focuses hugely on the academic progress of her children through strict schooling and many extracurricular activities. The

Tiger Mom is so called for her distinct 'hyper-disciplined' parenting approach and her laser-like focus on her children's achievements and performance. Needless to say, the Tiger Mom is often considered to be pushy. Chua describes back-to-back piano lessons, music classes and extensive ballet courses consuming most, if not all, of her non-study 'free time' every week. This strict scheduling was intended to help 'keep your children on track' to 'becoming all they could be'.

Though an extreme example, this is essentially a common position parents take when it comes to rationalising their expectations of their children, but pressuring a child to 'be all that they can be' is a fairly ambitious expectation. How many of us adults can claim to 'be all that we can be'? This attitude fails to take into account the realities of life, particularly children's lives, and the general principles of performance. No athlete achieves their best every week. There is a natural ebb and flow to performance that fluctuates because of circumstances, and the notion of having 'off days' and not performing at an optimum level is part of life. Yet there are parents who do not grasp this concept and who expect their children to perform at their peak all the time.

The typical GAA Tiger Mum has this drive for perfect performance and has overwhelming expectations for their children. The reason I have chosen mothers and not fathers for this example is because Amy Chua's book has spurred on the debate about mothers. I use the GAA as an example because it is an amateur sport, so there's no 'big leagues' in terms of fame and fortune. Certain activities have traditionally featured extraordinary pressure to perform, such as ballet, gymnastics, swimming or playing a classical instrument. These are the usual choices of Tiger Moms for their children as they demand hours of practice and have strict criteria for what is good enough. Yet this phenomenon has become so widespread that it is now creeping into other more amateur sports and hobbies that previously would not have featured this kind of approach. It is well documented that children's sporting clubs are finding it increasingly difficult to manage the behaviour of over-zealous parents on the sidelines, who can be seen shouting obscenities at officials and opposing players. Young people regularly describe the ferocious pressure to perform from demanding parents. Perhaps this is a vicarious re-living of parents' own lost experiences in childhood that they are now working out through their intense engagement with their children. Perhaps it's part of an intense desire to keep up with the Joneses. Whatever the explanation, this approach can over-stimulate children by focusing them too heavily on one highly structured, pressurised activity or by overwhelming them with too many of them.

In these highly pressured situations, children can become overwhelmed. Relentless training and extracurricular schedules mean that children have little or no time for free play. Without free time, children's capacity to entertain themselves can be inhibited as they can struggle to be alone and unoccupied. In cases where a GAA Tiger Mum is also directly involved in the organisation of the sporting activity, this can be even more difficult for their child, as their peers and teammates will see the demanding parent at work, pressuring their child to perform. A friend and colleague of mine, who runs a local football team, was once offered €200 by a player's mother to make sure her son had a place on the team every week for the whole season. Some children's teams have had to organise a 'silent sideline' rule in order to deal with aggressive parents.

Encouraging your child to get involved in activities and supporting them to do their best is by no means a bad thing. However, when a child's performance disappoints their parent, it can have a huge impact on the child. I have witnessed lots of fallout from parents being too involved or too emotionally invested in their children's sporting or extracurricular activities. Extreme parental drive for performance with the focus solely on the final outcome can have a very damaging impact on children's self-esteem, self-worth and sense of validation. Scheduling too many activities can overwhelm children and leave them unable to spend time alone, amuse themselves or relax.

It is understandable that you want your child to do well in whatever they do. However, if this wanting them to do well morphs into a need for them to be the best – for you or your child – then you've got a problem! Later in the book, I will describe ways that you can manage this urge to push your children excessively and will look at the difficulties inherent in the desire to 'be all that we can be'.

Trampoline envy

During the Boom, many families had more disposable income than they do now to spend on their families, whether it was for homes, cars, private schools, family holidays or children's activities. Children who were born into that era in Ireland are known as the 'Celtic Tiger Cubs'. These children became accustomed to living in households with money to spare, and the combination of this with an indulgent M50 Parent dynamic meant that large portions of parents' disposable income was spent on their children, in the form of hobbies, activities and education.

For me, the trampoline (of all things) has become a symbol of both the economic boom and the bust that followed. One day after the recession hit, I was speaking to two parents who were trying to describe how they 'didn't go mad in the Boom', something I hear a lot. By way of explanation, one parent went on to say, 'We had a very modest lifestyle up to now. Sure, we didn't even have a trampoline.' This phrase stuck in my head. Somehow, the trampoline (which, in my childhood, was an item limited to fancy schools with expensive gym halls or cool play areas designed for the whole community) had become a must-have household status symbol. In the '80s it might have been a Soda Stream or a Space Hopper, but in Ireland in the 2000s it was a 12-foot trampoline in your back garden.

I often get asked about the effect of the recession on children, and my answer has always been that it certainly has an effect. Children are not responsible for coping with redundancy, jobseeker's allowance or meeting large mortgage repayments, but they are affected by our stress and their own. Although many families go to considerable lengths to shield their children from any financial changes in the household, children still notice. Parents sometimes have to work two or three jobs to pay private school tuition fees for their children, and parents usually work incredibly hard to protect their children from their misguided financial choices or pure bad luck. Despite their parents' most valiant efforts, children in families hit by the recession have not been immune to their parents' anxieties. Children who discuss these issues with me in therapy often ask that I not report these conversations back to their parents, as they feel they have enough on their plate.

Adjusting to a new lifestyle is difficult for many parents; it is also difficult for children. Children can soak up tense atmospheres in the family home without knowing the exact details of the situation, which can lead them to imagine a worst-case scenario that far outstrips reality. Children often harbour lots of worries without being able to articulate them adequately. Sometimes children act out in response to anxiety and become more testing for their parents. As ever, it is important for parents to look for the meaning behind these behaviours.

Young people are also exposed to the mainstream media, which seem to talk relentlessly about unemployment and economic hardship. Some internalising children can ruminate over these concerns and worry for their own futures; with older children, this places a lot of pressure on getting good marks in school. They might be considering attending university and whether there will there be a job for them at the end of it, or whether they will have to emigrate to find work. Their friends may be leaving.

It is not advisable to burden children with the ins and outs of your financial strife, but to shelter children from these realities may not be helpful either. It is important that you explain your situation to children in a way that they *can* understand and manage, because much of what causes any of us anxiety is the fear of the unknown and unpleasant surprises are upsetting to everyone. One child told me that the first time he realised that things were bad was when he came home and a man was at the door looking to see about the trampoline that was on Done Deal. The boy was confused. His mother came to the door and showed the man outside to the back garden. After about 20 minutes the boy saw the man fold up the trampoline and put it in the back of his van. The boy was upset by this and what it meant for his family. His mother felt bad when she saw this, so she bought him a smaller trampoline later that week. But the boy noticed that his mum had stopped going to the spinning class that he knew she once enjoyed. He said he could never enjoy using the new trampoline after that, because he knew what it had cost his mum to buy it. He had been crestfallen on the day it was sold, not because of the trampoline itself, but because he didn't know what was going on. In this case, it seems that if his mum had talked to him about it, he would gladly have given up his toy to help the family cause.

Children can be wise beyond their years, and more generous than we might expect; other children have told me that they would have happily changed from their fee-paying school to a state school if it meant that they saw more of their dad, who was working two jobs to pay their tuition. In communicating with our children about serious concerns like the family finances, we can better judge where they are in terms of developing good sense and strong values – and they might just surprise us.

The risk-free childhood

A 'play den' (which goes by many names, but which I'm sure is a kind of facility that many of you know well) is a large warehouse-type building full of soft furnishings, slides, nets, climbing frames, ropes, ball pools and the like. Its purpose is to provide children with a safe yet adventurous environment in which they can play and explore. Many parents use these facilities for holding birthday parties for large groups of children or just in the general run of weekend activities to entertain their children.

I've spoken to a lot of parents who are big fans of these kinds of facilities, but as a parent and a psychotherapist I will state from the outset that I am not. I can understand the appeal of play dens: given the awful Irish weather, outdoor activities are not always possible, so an indoor playground sounds like a wonderful idea. But the indoor play den is fundamentally different from the traditional playground. These warehouses are set up in such a way that the soft furnishings give the illusion that no one can get hurt. Rather than fostering children's curiosity, they encourage reckless abandon. Play dens are largely unregulated, without any trained staff in the enclosures, and most of the time parents struggle to actually see their children. Parents are usually instructed to sit well away from the play area in a café, where they are encouraged to sip over-priced cups of bad coffee or tea. A traditional outdoor playground offers a much better vantage point for parents to observe how their children interact with and relate to other children. I am not advocating that you be overly involved in your children's relationships or activities, but for very young children I believe that being able to at least see them is a reasonable expectation.

Play dens cater for very large groups of children of very different ages, who are often mixed together. This usually serves only to reward physically dominant children. On the few occasions I have been to one, each time I've spotted one large, brutish child holding court over most of the activities inside the enclosure. Furthermore, play dens are extremely loud and chaotic places where there are no rules posted on any walls bar an instruction to remove your shoes. No structure or organisation is encouraged, and even the concept of queuing and taking turns is often bypassed. The only point when a parent's attention is drawn to their child is if they have been hurt, have become upset or are stuck in a tube or slide somewhere and cannot get down.

I am a big fan of play. Play is a developmentally essential activity for children, and we need to have more places where children can develop their freedom of imagination and their physical strength. But the play den is not the answer, because it doesn't tick enough boxes for what play can do for children. In terms of encouraging decision-making and problem-solving and of developing a sense of cop on, the play den falls way short. Its soft furnishings fail to teach any sense of personal safety, which is crucial to exploration and good decision-making. Learning from older children isn't possible, because there aren't any rules or structures to understand in the chaos. Play in a play den isn't collaborative, because it moves at the speed or whim of the strongest child.

Fail better: the learning curve of being a parent

As should be clear by now, this is not a 'step-by-step guide' to creating the perfect child. In fact, it is perhaps the opposite of that: a realist's guide for the imperfect parents of imperfect children. I am very critical of many of the books on parenting that present an 'ideal' or 'foolproof' way to raise your children. Books that uphold these ideal scenarios add to the pressures modern society already places on parents, using fear as their marketing strategy.

This is not a 'step-by-step guide' to creating the perfect child. In fact, it is perhaps the opposite of that: a realist's guide for the imperfect parents of imperfect children.

I read some of the books aimed at parents-to-be as the prospect of fatherhood loomed in my own life. Many of these publications, often directed at mothers, paint a hazy, rose-tinted picture of the doting mother, sitting in a rocking chair, gazing lovingly into her sleeping infant's eyes and glowing with the wonder of it all. The message I took from my reading was that if I followed the methods contained in these books this image would be my reality. Soon, I was driving up the Naas Road at 5 a.m. trying to get a colicky baby to stop screaming, and it hit me just how inaccurate these images could be. Colic notwithstanding, in the great majority of cases, these books are simply not representative of any real-life parenting situation. 'What harm?' I hear you say, but these publications can be seriously unhelpful. All that I had read about being a parent before I became one focused on how to do it perfectly, under perfect circumstances. When the time came, and my child screamed from 4 p.m. to 6 a.m. non-stop despite my following what the book had told me to do, I felt like I was doing something horribly wrong.

The parenting ideals that these books sell to us often run the risk of knocking our spirit when we're down due to lack of sleep, overwhelmed and over-tired, further hindering our attempts to do what we can. After all, we typically read these books *before* we've had children, when we look at them as a kind of owner's manual, or we buy them to 'solve' a specific problem we've already had for some time. The sales pitch that being a parent is easy if you follow the instructions makes admitting that you are struggling even harder.

I regularly speak to parents about their experiences of the early days of their children's lives, and I am continually told about mothers' struggles with post-natal depression that was left untreated or undetected for long periods of time after their children were born. When I ask these women why they waited to tell anyone, they all say similar things: 'I didn't know what it was' or 'Everyone told me it was normal and to "get on with it".' More worryingly, others say that they were ashamed and could not bring themselves to tell anyone.

It is so common for mothers and fathers who are struggling with being parents not to feel able to admit their struggles. They are 'blessed' with this 'bundle of joy' and don't feel they can complain that it's hard. From the get-go, parents are under pressure to get it right, without taking into account the real-life challenges that often make getting it right very difficult, if not impossible. A significant number of women report having post-natal depression for the first one to two *years* of their child's life, so the notion that 'struggling on' is the best thing to do is just not correct. Those formative years are so important for both parent and child, and many attachment theorists suggest that the 'hard-wiring' of a child's personality is developed in that crucial period. To try to raise a child when either you or your partner is under a cloud of depression naturally affects how that process unfolds, so I urge all new parents who feel they are struggling to ditch the books and talk to someone.

Parents are not always the problem, but they are always part of the solution.

From the outset, I want to state that I see parenting as a 'task of failure'. Don't worry: this isn't as negative as it sounds. It's simply important to understand that as parents we will all fail, perhaps in many aspects of what we do with our children. But our goal should be to avoid some of the possible pitfalls of raising children today. First, we must look at ourselves and address our own issues as adults. Once we have done that, we can examine the effects of these patterns of behaviour on our parenting styles and consequently on our relationships with our children.

It is also important to acknowledge that each child is different and needs to be raised differently. As parents, we need to account for what we can do with our children and, more importantly, what we cannot. One of the main differences that separates one child from another is their individual temperament. As parents, we can only help our children to manage their temperaments better, no matter what it may be. Whether your child is mild-mannered and passive, fiery and highly emotional or somewhere in between is a significant factor in the outcome for any child. Even with aspects of a child's personality that fall more on the 'nature' side of the divide, there's plenty of 'nurturing' you can do to help them along. A colleague of mine with whom I worked in Edinburgh used to always say to me, 'Parents are not always the problem, but they are *always* part of the solution.' Parents are not always guilty of misguided parenting if their child's behaviour takes a worrying turn, but there is always something that they can do to help. Parents can learn to understand these difficulties and to assist their child in learning to cope, manage or respond to them.

More generally, as parents we need to take into account

that many aspects of our lives are beyond our control, so dwelling on our missed opportunities or questionable choices in raising our children is futile. Instead, we must think about how best to support our children, whatever kind of children they may be.

WHY COP ON, AND WHY NOW?

So we're determined to do right by our children, and to raise them as well as we can, even though it might be a rocky road. We may be stretched in terms of time, money, childcare, energy or inspiration, or we may struggle with only a few of those things, but our children all have one thing in common: if they are to be happy and healthy in our busy, distracting modern world, they're going to need to have their feet firmly planted on the ground – and they need us to show them how it's done.

Children need to understand their own value, the importance of their family and friends, and to learn in time how to overcome life's trials and tribulations. For this, they need cop on.

What is 'cop on'?

This purely Irish colloquialism is both a verb and a noun, something that we do ('to cop on') and something that we have and need to hold on to. Cop on is something that Irish people value, so it's used as a command when people are acting irrationally or immaturely – 'Would you ever cop on!' or, better still, 'Cop on to yourself!' – and we admire it in those who are level-headed: 'She's far too copped on for that nonsense.'

It's in the positive construction that the true value of cop on lies. For me, cop on is the ability to be rational, resilient and sensible, and to have a bit of grit. Among my aspirations for my own children, cop on ranks highly on the list. Children with a good deal of cop on can be trusted to make sensible decisions when the need arises and to handle tasks that might challenge them a little bit. In a time when parents' supervision of their children's physical activity and whereabouts has never been so tight, but when their regulation of their children's online communication is frequently very loose, cop on is an absolute must to instil in our children. Cop on incorporates all kinds of the skills and qualities that academic journals describe as 'emotional intelligence', 'resilience', 'self-awareness' or 'adaptive decision-making'.

If you decide to raise your child to have a good degree of cop on, it will determine many of the decisions that you will have to make about them as they grow up. If you succeed, it will make them more capable of making good choices themselves.

When parents ask me at what age they should let their children have, say, a mobile phone, be alone in the house or start school, I always say that it depends on the child. This is because age is an arbitrary way to define development; the two are often, but certainly not always, related. When I say, 'It depends on the child', I am referring essentially to cop on. A 13-year-old with a good degree of cop on is often a better bet for unsupervised internet access than a 17-year-old with very little cop on. Age here is irrelevant; the quality you're looking for is that they will have the cop on to hit the 'back' button or tell someone if they find themselves in trouble or in a compromising situation.

When your child is inevitably offered the opportunity to do something they shouldn't, likely as not you won't be there.

When your child is inevitably offered the opportunity to do something they shouldn't, likely as not you won't be there. These are the very moments that your child's decision-making abilities will be put to the test. You'd like them to have the cop on to know how to make the right decision, no matter how unpopular it may make them. The ability to contextualise a situation, think rationally about it, weigh up the possible gains versus the possible consequences and make a decision is obviously hugely important to how your children live their lives.

But cop on is about more than good decision-making in the heat of the moment; it defines how we manage situations, good or bad, in the medium and long term. Your child will more than likely sit a state exam; the degree of cop on they possess will determine whether they approach it with a detrimental level of perfectionism or put in a strong effort to do as well as they can while maintaining a sense of perspective. With your help, they will have enough cop on to value the work they put into it and what it taught them beyond the outcome, and realise that exam results do not define them, for good or bad. Your child will also most likely be dumped by a boyfriend or girlfriend at some stage in their lives. Their response to this event will be determined by their ability to, over time, contextualise the relationship, evaluate the situation for what it is and come to accept that the break-up is unfortunate but something they can bounce back from eventually.

So cop on informs our ability to make decisions and to react appropriately to situations. Simple enough, but to raise children with cop on we must first ensure that they have some basic tools.

Copping on: getting a sense of sense

The developmental trajectory through childhood and adolescence varies so much from person to person that it is impossible to reliably assign an age to the appropriateness of any activity. There is a vast difference between a 12-year-old and an 18-year-old in all areas of responsibility, and the six-year gap at this life stage is far more significant than it is in adulthood. How much sense a child has plays the most important part in determining the age at which they can manage a particular level of responsibility.

So how do we define 'sense'? For me, sense comes from an accumulation of a number of attributes and influences. Elements such as maturity, resilience, temperament and self-esteem are cornerstones of measuring sense and are important factors in how we make responsibility-related decisions for our children.

The phenomenon that we describe as cop on or sense is one of the most crucial aspects of a child's development. It is one of the best forms of protection a child can develop, and it will stand to them for the rest of their lives. Some of the qualities required for developing good sense are out of our – and even sometimes our children's – control, like temperament and personality. Other qualities, like resilience, good self-worth and cop on certainly are things we can encourage. As I will show, the way children interact with the world today can negatively affect their capacity to develop these skills, so we as parents must counteract these influences by nurturing good sense in our children.

Let's look at how we can support our children in being more resilient and robust in managing life's challenges.

WHAT WE NEED: DEVELOPING GOOD RELATIONSHIPS AND GOOD SENSE

Now, more than ever, we need to ensure that we have strong, well-developed relationships with our families. All families, whatever their circumstances or their daily routines, can benefit from building the basics of good communication.

Beginning to develop a lexicon of emotional words is very useful to children; rather than acting out, they will have the tools to articulate how they feel.

Beginning to develop a lexicon of emotional words is very useful to children; rather than acting out, they will have the tools to articulate how they feel – though they may do that too. This is particularly relevant with younger children, as common behavioural concerns related to sleeping, bed-wetting and eating can be symptoms of psychological distress that they do not have the capacity to put into words.

Providing children with the language to discuss their feelings is the first step in fostering their 'emotional intelligence', which will stand them in good stead in the future, when as an adolescent or adult they need to be pro-active about their needs or their mental health. Remember, *where words fail, behaviour takes over.* We can spot that in our own lives when we resort to shouting or groaning when frustration wins out and words just don't quite cover it. Adults can also get physical when words fail them, just like children; anyone who has ever assembled a bookcase with an Allen key for an hour, only to realise that they've done it wrong and need to start again and resort to kicking it can tell you that. A young child who hits out at their parents when they remove a toy the child wanted to continue to play with is the same: the child lacks the language to argue their case for keeping the toy or communicate their exasperation at it being removed, so they lash out. With this in mind, it is important to provide children with words for emotions so as to minimise the potential for behavioural expressions.

We must make a point to explain to our children that their emotions can be – and should be – both positive and negative. This will not only allow our children to identify when they are feeling sad or worried but will also make them mindful of when they feel positive emotions like happiness and pride. This sense of balance fosters an improved awareness of themselves and their environment and goes a long way in allowing them to be more resilient and to develop a sense of cop on. Knowing ourselves and our feelings better encourages a sense of value and meaning; with the ability to express their emotions, our children can learn to prioritise and contextualise experiences, and respond in a proportionate way to events in their lives, both positive and negative.

For me, the most important job of a parent is to learn to understand your child, their behaviour, their emotions and why they think the way they do. In my clinical work I constantly fine-tune the methods I use to understand the young people who attend, the environments that they come from, the difficulties that they face and the inner mechanisms of their emotions. These are the sorts of tools I use.

Creating a relationship of openness

When I talk with young people about their difficulties, I always remind myself that the purpose of the interaction is not for me to provide them with answers, but to provide an understanding of their problems. The experience of feeling 'misunderstood' is common in child and adolescent development, and it is important that children and adolescents learn to manage the frustration inherent in feeling misunderstood. It is important that we allow young people to experience feeling misunderstood first hand, as it teaches them to express their views, values and beliefs more clearly. If they have to consider how to approach others, and how to go about putting their feelings into words, they will reach a more nuanced understanding of how they feel. This kind of clarity is traditionally achieved as children progress towards adulthood.

'My parents just don't get it' is a phrase I hear a lot when working with young people. What it is to 'get it' has always interested me. Sometimes parents are accused of 'not getting it' when they simply don't agree with their children, but more often than not it's a question of a perceived gap in a parent's understanding of their child's circumstances or of why their child holds the view they do. Naturally, children see the world through a very different lens than their parents; they always have, and likely always will.

Rather than your just accepting this to be the case, however, there is a value in you trying to narrow this divide as much as possible in order to strengthen your relationship with your children. What's called for is a meeting of minds, so that you and your children can begin to see things from each other's perspective. Merely understanding your children's worries, fears and sadness can go a long way towards helping them. Once another person's perspective is understood and accepted it becomes evident almost immediately within a relationship. This new, improved understanding creates more effective communication, fewer crossed wires and a closer relationship. Trying to understand *why* young people do what they do is far more effective than trying to fix their behaviour. What I have realised is that, more often than not, young people actually don't want to be fixed. Instead, first and foremost, they want to be heard.

The less you listen, the more I have to shout!

If we agree that communication is the key to any good relationship, then we can place a value on listening and feeling heard in our relationships with our children. In my experience, if a young person does not feel heard at home, it has a significant impact on their openness and relationships. Some young people withdraw; others may begin to communicate in indirect ways through acting out. Once you have promoted the emotional intelligence and self-awareness of your child, your next challenge is communicating with them once they have the words or the language. This also requires a degree of mutual insight in order to be carried out optimally.

Parents often need help in learning how to listen to their

children in order to really hear what they have to say. This is a very tricky concept to grasp, and, understandably, in most cases it is initially met with a degree of defensiveness. Parents often ask if listening to their children just means letting them do everything their way. But listening to your children means giving them a voice to practise asserting their own views in a way that is neither overly passive nor overly aggressive. The listening process allows your child to be heard and acknowledged, but it doesn't mean you have to agree with them; this is the most important distinction. Of course allowing children to do as they please without any rules or consequences has no value, as it doesn't teach them how to regulate their behaviour, nor does it demonstrate the cause and effect of their actions. As a result, they miss out on developing core aspects of cop on.

Towards developing cop on, it is important that children see a value in expressing their views. Doing so should validate their feelings. As a parent, you need only encourage openness; you don't need to be excessively lenient. Like all of us, children will consider communicating their views to be worthwhile when they think they will get a 'fair airing'. Some children also find talking through their opinions and desires with their parents to be 'containing', a concept I'll discuss later in this section. Even a child who wants more autonomy and control may find that talking through their issues with a parent is enough, as some children who outwardly demand control may unconsciously be crying out *to be* controlled. Regardless of the outcome, if you talk to and listen to your child, they will know that they have been heard, and may in time see your final decision in context – but this takes some cop on to achieve.

For example, when I was a pre-teen, there were four of us who hung around in a group. Three of us were always being called indoors once our curfew was reached. One member of the group, however, seemed to be allowed to stay out as long as she wanted. I remember feeling so jealous of my friend's 'cool' parents, who allowed her such freedom. I met that friend many years later and learned that she had been envious of us three who were reliably called in at a minute past curfew – because our parents 'cared'.

The value of listening to your children can be misinterpreted as an encouragement to 'get down with the kids' and become like a peer to them. Some think the approach of being a 'trendy parent' encourages your children to confide in you. In my experience, this doesn't always work. Parents do not need to be like their children; they just need to show that they are open to understanding the challenges their children face, which goes a long way to being a parent who 'gets it'. Besides, the reality is that young people do not want their parents to be their friends; most of them have enough friends. Young people want and need their parents to be their parents, to love, support and guide them as they learn how to make good choices for themselves.

If you think your efforts to understand your child might be in vain, think again: I often hear young people say things like 'My mum doesn't understand, but I know she's trying to.' Young people really can and do value effort over outcome sometimes, and, with luck, this is the value system that you have instilled in them. Once you have made the effort to listen – and hopefully having been given some credit for it by your children – you can deal more holistically with your child's specific problems as they occur, addressing them in the context of your child's particular situation rather than in isolation.

OK, so I don't have to 'be' them; I just have to 'get' them. How do I get them?

Being willing to engage with your child's world is a good start in learning how to understand it. This may seem incredibly obvious, but you would be surprised how regularly people struggle to be open-minded. Whether the stakes are high – world politics, religion, social injustices – or relatively small – children acting out, teenagers being unreasonable – trying to understand another person's perspective is a good start to ending conflict, but it can be tricky to do.

No matter what age your child is, they will experience stress and trauma as they make their way through life and the level of that stress is very real to the child, even if, from your adult perspective, it's doesn't seem like a big deal. One of the most important things you as a parent can do is to try to empathise with your child, not only with regard to the circumstances of their problem but also with regard to their *perception* of those circumstances. If we trivialise our children's problems, we're telling them that these 'dramas' are not meaningful to us. Essentially, we're expecting our children to respond to a problem from an adult's perspective, which is unfair and ineffective.

To belittle a child's problem doesn't make the problem more manageable; it makes the child feel like you're not listening when they need your help. Whether it's a two-year-old who is reluctant to use her potty or a 14-year-old with an unrequited crush, the approach is the same. In psychotherapy we refer to this as 'getting down to the child's level'. By doing this, we are able to gain an insight into the experience of the child and to explore the different factors affecting how they are feeling and thinking. While we are down at this level, we can try to take a moment to consider where the child is in terms of their development and how this might affect the situation. For instance, to tell the anxious toddler to 'just use the potty because she needs to do it if she wants to go to play school' doesn't address the child's anxiety and only adds further pressure. Likewise, to tell a teenager who won't get out of bed because his girlfriend broke up with him to 'stop being ridiculous' only makes him feel misunderstood and more alone.

Trying to establish what lies behind your child's behaviour, in order to see what is going on at a deeper level, is far more effective in helping them to change that behaviour. This involves asking your child to tell you about their experiences and listening to their perspective of events, the impact of these events on their life and the hopes or worries they have for their future. By listening with an open and understanding ear, you can gain insight into your child's perception of their reality, or, in other words, their 'truth'. This truth may indeed contradict your truth – and that's okay. It is only important that you let your child know that you *understand* their experience; you do not have to agree with it. The most important element of this interaction is that your child feels that they've been heard. These deeper conversations help children feel able to navigate their own emotional world and may in turn help them to understand themselves better.

Regulating: a core task of adolescence

Emotional regulation, and regulation in general, is a key part of children's development. When a toddler in a shop rolls around the floor screaming and kicking because their parents wouldn't buy them chocolate buttons, we understand. One would hope that by the time they reach adulthood their reaction to disappointment would be more tempered and considered. As we grow up, we learn to regulate our responses to all sorts of things, including our sleep, diet and communication. A ten-year-old doesn't always know when he has had enough sweets before he gets sick; a 14-year-old at a sleepover doesn't consider how tired she will be the next day when she stays up talking until 5 a.m. Knowing when enough is enough is a skill normally acquired with age, so it makes sense that an adult hearing about a teenager waking up at three in the morning to check their Facebook page assumes it's lunacy, but a 25-year-old who is doing much the same thing perhaps doesn't. Later on in this book, I will discuss ways in which parents can promote regulation in the face of a culture that is seemingly hell-bent on challenging common sense.

Learning to wait

Waiting is an underrated skill that has many spin-offs in terms of learning. Old-fashioned though it sounds, learning to wait teaches us to value things when they arrive; it shows us that we can suffer through adversity and survive. Crucially for today's world, learning to wait also allows us a few moments to ourselves, which can be an opportunity for us to get to know ourselves; we can let our minds wander, think about something that's been bothering or inspiring us, or see what in our surroundings might catch our eye, perhaps discovering an interest in something – or someone – new. If we never learn to wait, we may never learn to be alone, and by never being alone, we limit our capacity to get to know ourselves.

As adults, we know from experience that although we may wait, and survive the waiting experience, we may be disappointed by what happens when the wait is over. You may have used your time waiting to weigh the possible outcomes for your wait in the immediate future at, say, the doctor's office. A lifetime of getting to know yourself in quiet moments will give you the inner resources to handle a positive outcome appropriately; it also teaches you how to handle a negative outcome, as you'll know that good things don't always come to those who wait.

Happiness is relative to expectations

Happiness and contentment are relative, and so there is sometimes an element of therapy that is not so much focused on making someone happier but rather on helping them to manage their expectations so they can achieve happiness in more realistic circumstances.

This is especially relevant with children and adolescents. Think about the child who receives 96 per cent in her spelling test. Initially, she is delighted – that is, until the child next to her gets 97 per cent. Then she feels devastated, upset she did not come first. Her 96 per cent is suddenly meaningless. Happiness, clearly, can be a fickle response to our expectations. Equally, as our expectations rise, so too can our unhappiness, anxiety and demand on ourselves. Discussing our expectations and the context of our reasons to be happy with our children can get them thinking independently about how to rate and manage their own happiness in time.

The society of discontent

Famously coined by Sigmund Freud in in the early twentieth century, the concept of the 'society of discontent' is still valid today. Far be it from me to compare myself to the great Sigmund Freud, but I find myself returning to his idea of the relationship of happiness to expectation levels: as our expectations as a society rise to unrealistic levels, an epidemic of unhappiness is inevitable. Many of my young clients bemoan a 'typical' life by saying, 'Finishing school, going to college, getting a job, getting married and having kids – where's the fun in that?' To them, a life eerily similar to my own and that of so many other adults is somehow unacceptable – it's just 'not enough'. They are preoccupied with 'making a difference' or 'making an impression', which raises expectations to an unachievable level for most young people and chips away at their ability to cope with the realities of life at the same time.

I reported this back to an older colleague of mine, one who would not be known for his sensitivity or open-mindedness. All he said was, 'Ah, for God's sake, Colman, they need to cop on.' I didn't think much of this at the time, but later I began to mull over this concept of 'cop on'. Parents I met often wished aloud that their child 'had more cop on' or that they could just tell their child 'to cop on'. These parents were frustrated with their children, yes, but maybe they were on to something. And so I began to explore the concept of cop on.

——

Forming an open, listening relationship with your children and teaching them how to communicate their feelings, use their inner reserves and manage their expectations are all key to the following five elements.

Yes, what follows is a 'how to', but not the sort that promises unreasonable results with little effort on your part. Building cop on in your children, and using cop on in your own approach to raising them, should be a constantly evolving process. In the sections below, I'll lay out the kinds of things you should keep in mind as you go.

The five elements I will highlight are drawn from some of the fundamental principles of child psychology. When put into practice in your daily family life, I hope they will help you to recognise, understand and ultimately meet your children's needs as they grow up to be copped-on young people.

WHERE TO BEGIN: FIVE STEPS TOWARDS RAISING COPPED-ON CHILDREN

In the same way that 'cop on' as a concept is difficult to describe, it is difficult to show parents how best to teach, develop, encourage and nurture it. However, when I was looking for a memorable way to frame the actions parents need to take in order to develop cop on in their children, I kept coming back to an old reliable concept in psychotherapy.

The 'Therapeutic Milieu' is a concept developed by the UK psychiatrist John Gunderson in the 1970s to describe the optimal therapeutic environment for individual growth and development. He identified five elements that are necessary for its creation. I am a great fan of Gunderson's Therapeutic Milieu model, and have developed various models of care around its five elements over the course of my career as a psychoanalyst. Since the publication of his five-element framework over 40 years ago, many theorists have used his principles for a variety of different purposes, but I don't think anyone has used the Therapeutic Milieu model to frame an approach to child-raising. Allow me to be the first.

I like the Therapeutic Milieu model approach so much because it is simple: it highlights in five words what needs to be in place for growth to occur. Its simplicity makes it particularly well suited to creating a parenting approach for busy families. Here, I have developed it to encourage a sense of resilience, robustness, personal growth and cop on in children, and I really hope that parents find it as helpful as I have, in both my professional and family life.

One of the reasons I decided to adapt the Therapeutic Milieu model in this way is that, after I became a parent, I found I *was* using these principles, much of the time unwittingly, in my relationships with my children and my approaches to parenting. The five elements or concepts here are accessible and useful; Gunderson simply describes five features or aspects of an environment that must be present in the right amounts in order for relationships to flourish. The five elements are containment, structure, support, validation and involvement.

Here I will explain what these terms mean and how they can be used in all aspects of parenting, but most importantly in the process of developing a sense of cop on in your child.

Containment

All environments must be contained. Think of a plastic box that serves to keep its contents from spilling everywhere and to keep its contents safe. In the Therapeutic Milieu model, the use of the term 'containment' refers more to a psychological containment than a physical one, but the basic idea is the same. At a fundamental level, children must feel cared for and must feel a parental presence in their lives in order to thrive; such an environment stops them from spilling out of control and keeps them physically and psychologically safe. I'm not talking about locking doors or containing a child within a defined physical space; psychological containment refers to having relationships that are stable and secure and that encourage growth. This is our most basic psychological need, because we can only develop, grow and emerge as healthy adults if we feel psychologically and emotionally safe as children.

This is our most basic psychological need, because we can only develop, grow and emerge as healthy adults if we feel psychologically and emotionally safe as children.

Children who lack psychological containment and don't feel safe will not feel able to express their emotions or feelings, and will therefore internalise them or express them through acting-out behaviours. Containing relationships are ones that encourage openness and honesty; they are non-judgemental and they put the contained person's interests first. As parents and adults, it is vital that our relationships with children are containing so that children feel safe enough to bring to us any issues or concerns that they have, safe in the knowledge that we will respond with their best interests at heart.

Containment also involves providing safe limits that protect children from themselves while they learn how to regulate their own behaviour and emotions. From infancy to young adulthood, emotional regulation is an ongoing process that children have to master as they develop, and your role in this process is to provide safe levels of freedom while preventing your child becoming overwhelmed and uncontained. Therefore, setting limits and gradually permitting increased levels of responsibility – in keeping with your child's level of cop on – is a core element of containment.

> *Setting limits and gradually permitting increased levels of responsibility – in keeping with your child's level of cop on – is a core element of containment.*

The best way to conceptualise containment is to think about somebody in your life who you feel that you can talk to about anything. This is the type of person who, if you rang in a time of need, regardless of the hour, would answer and respond in the best way possible. Their concern for you is entirely well intentioned; they have no ulterior motives and no sneaky background agendas. They will just listen to you, hear you and try to understand you in the best way that they can. They will provide you with an honest response, even if it sometimes means telling you that they are not in total agreement with your point of view or intended course of action. *This* is a containing relationship. For adults and children alike, a containing relationship allows us to feel safe enough to be open and to speak about what we are frightened of, what we worry about, and about the deepest concerns of our lives. Our intimate and serious feelings can only be articulated to someone who we know is there for us.

It is essential that your children have at least one containing relationship in their lives. It is considered an incredibly important aspect of their personal growth and development, and the presence of someone to act as a confidant or a non-judgemental role model cannot be underestimated.

These kinds of containing relationships give children and young people the opportunity to be open and honest and allow them the freedom to discuss anything. A core feature of a containing relationship between a child and an adult is the belief that the adult will not overreact or underreact to whatever the child brings to them; instead they will listen, hear and try to understand the child's experience and be there for them. This becomes more important as the child gets older and life becomes more complex.

As identified by the 'My World Survey', the largest study of young people in Ireland, one of the things that best protects the good mental health of young people is the presence of 'one good adult' in their lives. 'One good adult' is another way to describe a containing relationship, but the adult *does not necessarily have to be a parent*. They can be an older cousin, an aunt or an uncle or even a teacher or family friend. Parents of course prefer that it be one of them, but it is more important that this role is filled well than that it is filled by a parent. At times, the nature of the events in a young person's life may make their relationship with their parents particularly sensitive – a divorce or separation, trouble with a sibling – so it can be very helpful for children to have another adult in their lives they can trust.

Containment and containing relationships between you and your child can be built by completing a series of developmental steps. How we respond to each of these developmental steps is hugely important to the continuing growth of your relationship. Development begins long before your child is old enough to speak about complicated events in their lives: from the moment that they are born. There is a lovely expression that the renowned psychoanalyst Wilfred Bion uses to describe the very beginning of a containing relationship with a baby, when he describes the mother 'holding the child in her gaze'. This illustrates how containment and that unique feeling of safety are present from the very start and need to be nurtured and developed throughout your child's life. All that is required is for you to establish an openness and an approachability that lets your child know that you are there for them, no matter what the circumstances or the issue at hand.

It is crucial that the process of containment is a focus of your parenting from the outset. What I have learned in my experiences of working with young people and their families is that the time you invest in your parent-child relationship early on will pay dividends down the line when it comes to raising mature and copped-on young people.

Containment and cop on

In the course of my therapeutic work, I have heard many children describe experiences with their parents that are *not* examples of a containing relationship at work. Take a simple example: a child comes home to his parents and something is wrong. As it happens, he's being bullied, but he is unsure how to address the issue, so he begins to drop clues. In the course of their busy lives full of distractions, his parents miss the hints their child is dropping. His parents are tired from working long hours, or haven't lifted their heads from their smartphones, and thus haven't shown him they are interested in what he's trying to say. Whatever the reason, the child does not get a sense that his worries are being heeded, so he tries another method to manage them. This might take the form of developing more challenging behaviours, like picking an argument with a sibling or answering back in order to get his parents' attention. Alternatively, the child might utilise more passive ways of communicating his distress by reporting recurrent tummy pains or even developing eating difficulties.

Another example: consider a young girl who is having a problem at her gymnastics lessons. She seems to be very good and has a lot of potential, but she feels that she's under too much pressure. She isn't enjoying gymnastics as much any more, as it's now all about winning. On hearing this, her father jumps straight to criticism: she's being lazy and has been spending too much time talking about boys and playing with her phone. Her father relishes his daughter's success, so he starts telling her what to do: socialise less, concentrate more and 'suck it up' when it comes to the aspects of gymnastics she doesn't enjoy. This reaction is uncontaining because the father does not succeed in making his daughter feel that she has been heard. Instead, she feels weak and foolish, or worse, invisible to her father because he hasn't acknowledged her experience or point of view on the situation. In this situation, an externalising child may well resist their father's advice and become more difficult. An internalising child may now begin to 'throw' competitions or play up an injury to avoid being successful in the hope of being heard that way. When a child's attempt to communicate isn't acknowledged, it won't go away.

It is often very difficult to respond appropriately when we

hear that our children are having problems. This is simply a reflection of how passionately and totally we love our children. A perfect example is the enthusiastic father who proudly claims that if any child in the school yard or on the football pitch harms a hair on his child's head, 'I will go straight down there and sort it out.' This declaration is not a containing one, despite the father's best intentions. Instead, his child hears that if he is bullied and he comes to his father with his problem, he's going to have a knee-jerk reaction that will only serve to aggravate an already difficult situation. So, for fear that his father will make a bad situation worse, in this scenario the child has no confidence in his father's capacity to be containing so he goes on to conceal that he is being bullied for many more months.

Another example of a non-containing response is when parents over-burden children with freedom or power. Children who are permitted to watch TV or play computer games in their rooms until all hours of the night may not be able to manage this degree of responsibility and may become over-tired and begin to push boundaries and be disruptive. In my experience, many of these children are crying out to be contained, and their problematic behaviour may well be a symptom of this appeal.

The art of being a containing parent is not something that can be executed perfectly every time. Most parents live very busy lives and it is inevitable that, on occasion, some of your children's concerns will fall through the cracks. As with all the approaches to raising children that this book will look at, it's not about doing it perfectly; instead, it's about trying to keep the basic concept of containment in mind when our children need help. We just have to remind ourselves of the value of containment in the development of our children's self-esteem and their ability to problem-solve and be heard. The challenge is that modern life presents so many distractions and quick-fix possibilities that are not only insufficient substitutes for containment but actively work against it. Containment is not about agreeing to everything that your child wants when they're struggling; it is merely about listening to whatever they have to say and trying to understand their views. You're not telling them what they want to hear; you're supporting them by helping them see their situation in a way that is rational, mature and sensible.

Offering this kind of support is also about limiting your child's desires so that the challenges they face are manageable for them. For example, if you already have a strong, supportive relationship with your 15-year-old, she might tell you that she wants to go out drinking with her friends. A containing parent will hear their daughter's desires and acknowledge the various pressures she's feeling to join her peers, and how hard it can be to stand your own ground in the face of such pressure. Even though the containing parent makes these concessions to their child, they can still make the decision that underage drinking is illegal and is a poor choice for their child, so it is not permitted. Even though this is a negative outcome for their child, it is a containing response, because the parent has heard what their child has to say while still making the correct judgement that, at 15 years of age, their child is not ready to manage alcohol responsibly. The containing parent is therefore making a decision to regulate their child's desires for the purposes of her safety. While this may not be aligned to the wishes or the desires of the child, it is still a containing response, because the parent is teaching their child the value of sensible decision-making – which again shows the relationship between containment and cop on.

Consider a child who is having difficulties because they are struggling with their sexuality. This initial conversation is often a difficult one for parents, and as a result is rarely one that is managed in a containing manner. However, where containment has been a cornerstone of the parent-child relationship the child will feel free enough to have that conversation in the first place – and open communication with their children is of course what most parents want.

Sometimes, particularly early on, there are occasions when being a containing parent can be hard, or even impossible, such as during a bout of post-natal depression, when parents are working long hours or when there is a close family bereavement. In these circumstances, the capacity of a parent to be emotionally available is compromised, but this should only be temporary. Such dips in attention to our children in extreme circumstances are perfectly normal, and all aspects of our relationships with them – including the containing relationship – can certainly be redeemed. We simply have to strive to improve the emotionally containing aspects of our relationships whenever we can.

> *If we want our children to develop resilience, problem-solving, sensible decision-making and good self-awareness, developing a containing relationship with them is the place to start.*

If we want our children to develop resilience, problem-solving, sensible decision-making and good self-awareness, developing a containing relationship with them is the place to start. Every child learns from observing the people around them and how they cope with their own life challenges; as a parent, you provide your child with the blueprint for how to cope with, respond to and manage life's challenges. Therefore, if containment is a feature of your approach to raising your child, your child will feel able to approach you with their challenges and you will be able to assist them to find the answers at a pace that they can manage.

The crucial part of containment is to gradually withdraw the degree of support as your child develops their own abilities to make good choices. This should be a carefully thought-out process that allows your child to stand on their own two feet and to use those same careful processes of considering and evaluating problems before making their decision. The ultimate goal of a parent is to become more or less redundant over time; when your child no longer 'needs' you, this is not a sign of failure but a measure of your success. Your child will always need you in some capacity, as sometimes there are challenges that age and time simply cannot cope with, but within reason.

Equally, it is important not to over-burden your child with responsibility as this too can disable their ability to cope. The pacing of containment will involve periods of intense containment and distant containment in relation to the child's age, ability and challenges. The pacing of this process is the key to its success. Your child's independence and individuation, when appropriately timed, is a milestone of parental success and one that should be celebrated, not lamented.

The ultimate goal of a parent is to become more or less redundant over time; when your child no longer 'needs' you, this is not a sign of failure but a measure of your success.

Structure

The second element of the five-element Therapeutic Milieu model – structure – is a really important aspect of parenting that is often discussed but is very hard to get right. It is widely accepted that structure decreases anxiety for people of all ages, and this is especially true in the case of children. It's logical enough: if children have structure to their days, they will know what is going to happen, when something will start and when it will end. This knowledge limits the possible outcomes of situations, which in turn curbs anxiety. This is especially true when it comes to an activity or life stage that children are finding uncomfortable. Children thrive when their lives are contained and structured, so long as this structure is reliable. All children learn through repetition, from their very earliest days. Any parent can tell you the benefits of a structured routine when you are trying to get an infant to sleep and the value of predictability for young children when it comes to daily routines like mealtimes and bedtimes. When structure is compromised or unreliable, children can become distressed and overwhelmed as they struggle to cope with these changes.

People, and especially children, naturally fear the unknown. Structure reduces anxiety in children simply by outlining what will happen and keeping them informed as much as is possible and appropriate for their developmental level, as in 'School is over, so I'll have a snack at home now before I go out to play.' Without the certainty of structure, children may not have the wherewithal to anticipate what might happen in the same way that an adult would, so a young child will likely get tired and cranky if after-school activities vary hugely from day to day.

A number of years ago, a boy had been referred to me for hyperactivity and the possibility of ADHD. I first spoke to his mother, who described a fairly tyrannical child. He was very over-active and destructive and had been getting into a lot of trouble in school. After I had got the boy's history, I went to fetch him from the waiting room, saying to him, 'Come with me now,' and he duly followed me into my office. We both sat down, and I saw a child who showed no level of hyperactivity but instead merely sat motionless and quite tearful in the chair opposite me. I started by asking him some simple questions about his age, class in school and the like, but he refused to answer. I suddenly became anxious that my questions were making this child feel worse. I briefly wondered if I had summoned the wrong child from the waiting room. He was so nervous that I went back to the waiting room to ask his mother to join us in the session, as I felt the boy was becoming increasingly anxious in my company. When she entered the room she took a seat and her son reached over and hugged her, whispering something in her ear. She turned to me and said, 'He thought you were taking him for ever.'

I realised that here was a young boy who had been behaving poorly in recent months and knew that he was seeing me as a result. I had just gone into the waiting room and told him that he had to come with me now. By this, he had understood that I was taking him from his mother for ever as a punishment for his bad behaviour and that he would never see his parents again. This was a stark example of my own inability to provide structure at a crucial moment for this boy. I had failed to indicate by my manner or by what I said what was expected of him. I didn't tell him how long I would be seeing him for, or whether our meeting was part of a long-term plan. It never occurred to me for a moment that he might think that I was now taking him away from his mother for ever. I learned a valuable lesson that day about creating even the most basic forms of structure for young people, and, as a rule, I now always indicate the length of time that a session will last to every young person that I meet.

A central task of child and adolescent development is regulation. Structure can have a considerable impact on a child's ability to regulate themselves and their behaviour. As with most things, children learn how to regulate themselves by watching their parents. As we know from watching children's behaviour, difficulties in regulating can lead to emotional responses that can be overwhelming to both parents and the children themselves, expressed through high levels of anxiety or difficult behaviour. The toddler who screams and shouts in the supermarket when she is not given a packet of chocolate buttons is a relatable example of the challenge of emotional regulation. The same goes for a teenager who reacts in a disproportionate way by screaming how much he 'hates' his parents, that they have 'ruined' his life by preventing him from attending a local disco. These challenges occur naturally across the full span of childhood and adolescence and are often just par for the course. But consistency in your approach as a parent – a consistent structure and a series of consistent messages – will help your child to internalise structure and learn how to regulate themselves. A consistently structured approach can be a really positive thing when well put together – but it's essential that you get the balance right.

In a young person's world, a great deal of their daily activity is highly structured. This is none more obvious than in school, where they have a starting time at, say, 8:30 a.m., a 'little break' at 11, a 'big break' at 12:30 and a finishing time at 3 p.m. Their lives are designed around timetables and they know these timetables inside out. These structures help young people to manage, plan and create a meaning in their day. If a similar order is provided in the context of a reliable family routine, then things like sleeping, eating and exercise can all be managed within appropriate limits. Typically, a good balance is achieved when there is a proportionate amount of time at home versus structured outside activities. Within these settings, there is the potential for even more structure regarding appropriate amounts of time with parents, time with friends, 'screen time', homework, study and free time.

Once in place, these structures, if managed well, will help your child to internalise their own structure and in turn manage their own anxieties. Your child will learn when is enough and will be able to identify when things are becoming too much. When children have a reasonable amount of time to themselves during a busy school week, they learn to acknowledge tiredness, to relax and to rest. They learn how to enjoy themselves during 'down time' and to appreciate the rules and cultures of more structured times. These skills are best developed when a child is given enough time and space in their day to be alone.

Getting the structure right

All this structure sounds like rather a lot, and of course it can be; when taken to an extreme, overly structured lifestyles for children can be more anxiety-ridden than a childhood that lacks structure. Children who spend almost all their post-school hours during the week in organised extracurricular activities can react badly. They can become either overly reliant on the timetabled activities to know what to do at any given moment and unable to amuse themselves, or they can become overwhelmed and simply exhausted by the excess of activity required of them.

Children who are raised without enough structure do not develop the skills of regulation, routine or self-limitation. Therefore, neither an overly structured environment nor an insufficiently structured environment is healthy for children's mental health. Once again, creating the right amount of structure and a sense of balance is all important in this process.

For parents, it is important to have a 'reliable' structure but not a 'rigid' structure; a reliable structure provides the kind of predictability your child needs but is flexible and responsive enough to meet the ever-changing needs of the family as a whole. Getting the structure right also depends on your child. Some children can manage their lives with relatively minimal structure and they're naturally comfortable in their own company and entertaining themselves, whereas other children may need decidedly more structure to their day in order to give them enough to do, particularly if they have lots of energy or lack motivation. Children who have a tendency to be anxious can often benefit from higher levels of structure too as they are comforted by reliability and punctuality which helps them feel secure in their environment.

Structure and cop on

First of all, the notion that we learn through repetition suggests that we can learn a great deal through a reliable structure. In their early years, the influence of structure can teach children to limit themselves by means of regular limits imposed by their parents. Take for example a toddler who becomes very fond of playing on his parents' iPad. His parents decide to set the time that he to is allowed to play on it, and they keep an eye on how he uses it and reward his good behaviour. They are consistent in applying this structure, so the child learns that if he adheres to the limits, he may be given more time on the device.

Teenagers who want to make their own decisions may benefit from a structured 'timeline of trust'. Let's say a teenager and his parents are debating a suitable curfew time over the summer holidays; the teenager thinks 11 p.m. is fair, while his parents feel that 9 p.m. is more acceptable. A trust timeline allows the teenager to be given the opportunity to earn his freedom in a structured way. His parents say that the curfew is 9 p.m. for the first night, but that for every night that the teenager is home on time and without a fuss, the curfew time will be extended by 15 minutes the following night. If the teenager is late or argues about being back at the agreed time, then the curfew will be reduced by 15 minutes the following night. This structured arrangement encourages the teenager to embrace responsibility and endorses the idea that the better he manages the freedom he has, the more freedom he will get.

This structured arrangement needs to be adhered to consistently if it is to be successful in encouraging sensible decision-making and working out the consequences of mature self-management. Keep in mind that structure is only as effective as the people who put it in place. Parents often complain that structured interventions have not worked, but when I examine the reasons for the failure with them, it usually turns out to be much more a problem with how the structure was implemented than with the plan itself.

As parents, we can stand back gradually as our children develop these skills. Structure, like containment, is a weaning process that can start out heavy-handed but requires a lighter touch as the child becomes more mature and copped on.

Support

The third element of Gunderson's model is exactly what it says on the tin: providing support for your children means that you are there for them, whatever the circumstances, to provide nurturance, guidance and love. Support does not have to mean providing for every single one of your child's needs yourself; it can mean you support them by getting them access to the help they need. Getting the degree of support right is hard, as you need to balance the amount of support so that your child does not feel smothered or so supported that they don't learn how to do things for themselves.

Support also changes: there are periods in children's lives when they require intensive support and other times when they may need less. Learning to share out different levels of support can be a dilemma for parents who have a number of children. Sibling rivalry can play a part here; children will argue that the 'favourite' child gets the most support, so parents often go to tremendous lengths to ensure parity. Though providing equal support to all your children at all times might seem like the right way to go about it, and though it may be what your children say they prefer, your children will require periods of more intensive support at different periods in their lives. In most cases this will even out over the span of childhood, say when a small child is experiencing separation anxiety when starting out at school or when a teenager is sitting a state exam. The levels of support you provide your children during these stressful life stages will naturally wax and wane according to their circumstances.

Unconditional support

The first question to ask yourself is whether your child experiences your support as support or as pressure. Some parents encourage their child to take part in a hobby or an extracurricular activity but don't show an interest in their ongoing efforts, and merely drop their child off at the activity. On the other hand, there are parents who become intensely involved in supporting their children's extracurricular activities and hobbies to the point of interfering. Here I am referring the GAA Tiger Mum, who becomes incredibly invested in their child's hobby, generally because their child displays a particular 'flare' for the activity. It is rare to see the same level of parental support if their child is decidedly average at the activity. This suggests that sometimes support is conditional on, in the first instance, the parent's own level of interest, and, in the second, the child being particularly talented. Either approach sends the wrong message to the child. As parents, we should support our children in every way, shape and form, regardless of their ability. Perhaps a child who is struggling to make the team and spends hours on the sidelines is the one who requires more support than a child who is swamped with medals and trophies for their achievements.

It is not just in the area of extracurricular or 'fun' activities that a child may need support. A child who has dyslexia or other learning difficulties may need that extra hour of homework and reading in the evening to reach the level of their classmates, and it is important that they be provided with extra support in a way that is encouraging and nurturing and allows them to understand that it is their effort itself that is important. Although doing an hour of spellings may seem far less appealing than watching your child win the Leinster Horse Riding Finals or the Regional Swimming Championships, it is just as important.

Alternatively, if you have a child who excels academically and is genuinely bored at school or a child who needs a bit of inspiration when it comes to enjoying particular school subjects, they will need your help in coming up with new, challenging things to do to fire up their imagination. Outings to the zoo, museums, films or whatever might inspire them and push their limits, which will encourage them to put in extra thought and effort in order to understand new subjects and experiences. There is no better way to drive home the importance of putting in the effort than by putting in the effort yourself.

In order to have the desired effect, our support should be unwavering and unconditional and each of our children should feel as supported as the next, depending on their circumstances.

Support and cop on

So what is the desired effect of cop on? When you choose to support an aspect of your child's life, you are showing your child that this particular feature of their life is important, and important to you. This will in turn inform what your child considers to be valuable. As a result, it is vital that you place value on truly worthy, lasting attributes, such as loyalty, kindness, support, respect, courtesy, affection and compassion. These meaningful and important qualities are often not valued enough in the school environment, which is a great pity – but all the more reason that they be a focus of family life.

That you support your child through difficult periods in their life tells them that they are valuable as a person, and it communicates your belief that their life is worthy of support and nurturance. *What* we place value on as parents we will pass on to our children, but if our support is too overwhelming or conditional, it may have an inverse effect. So the parent who places all their emphasis on supporting academic achievement will cause their child to adopt either a similar belief system or an entirely opposite one. An over-emphasis on academic achievement may cause their child to lose perspective and develop anxiety about school work; another child (even within the same family) may become overwhelmed by the level of expectation and buck against the parental pressure, becoming rebellious and under-achieving when it comes to school. As with all parenting matters, it helps to communicate with your children about how they're feeling if you think they're struggling. Parents of young people who are actively resisting all things school-related often feel that signing their child up for extra grinds is showing them support. The reality is that many young people experience this as further pressure and a form of conditional support and so continue their resistance to this value system.

If we want our children to develop cop on, then it is important that we as parents cop on to what is important. We must invest our time and effort into supporting the value systems that we want our children to adopt and lead by example. If you want your child to be a sensible decision-maker, try to be one yourself and, when appropriate, discuss your decision-making process with your children. Then support them in making sensible decisions in their own lives, and reward good decisions with further support to help them make more complex decisions.

A parent's support of their child is a life-long commitment. There is never a time when your supporting role is concluded; it merely changes focus. In other areas of parenting, the purpose of helping your child to develop is to gradually make your role redundant as your child becomes self-sufficient. So, in most cases, you have done your job as a parent when you are no longer needed. In the case of support, however, this is not true. As a parent, you need to provide and withdraw intensive support in keeping with what your child needs. Also, try to practise what you preach: if you want your child to have a measured view of the world and be able to respond in a measured way to all of life's events, be sure to let them see you doing the same, then support them to cope similarly in their own lives. Raising a child that values love, kindness, fairness and balance will be far easier if you support them using those same skills and acknowledge the importance of enduring qualities of good character, good sense and cop on.

Validation

For me, this is one of the most important elements of the Therapeutic Milieu model. Validation is one of the most underestimated aspects not only of being a parent but of life in general. In child psychology, we speak ad nauseam about the importance of qualities like self-esteem, self-worth and self-belief and of their role in maintaining good mental health in children. Validation is key to cultivating these qualities.

Validation is defined in psychological terms as the sense of being heard. This sense is vitally important to all of us, and we seek validation in all areas of our lives. As adults we seek validation in our workplace, in our family lives and from our partner; it is necessary throughout our lives, and at no point is it more important than during childhood and adolescence.

Visibility

Children can feel invisible in their school environment, in their relationships with their peers and even within their family. This feeling of invisibility is also related to each child's expectation of what counts as visibility. Some children demand a lot of attention, so their parents already feel that the child is the centre of family life, even though the child themselves may feel unimportant. This comes down to the concept of 'multiple truths': both are true. Although a parent may be running themselves ragged providing for their demanding child, if the child feels unimportant the parent needs to listen and find out why.

Validating your child's view is not the same as agreeing with them all the time, which is neither necessary nor effective in nurturing a sense of validation. Validation is not about being agreed with; it's about being heard. Teenagers make this mistake too. They can be genuinely shocked when, although you appear to be listening to them as they explain why they think it's a good idea to get their nose pierced, you still forbid them to do it. They are baffled that, although their point of view has been heard and you asked them questions about their motivations and listened to their answers – thus giving them validation – you still disagreed with them.

All that is required to give validation to your child is that you hear what their beliefs, thoughts and objectives are, and that you acknowledge and validate their feelings. This may mean trying to understand the peer pressure element of adolescent life or the desire to fit in and be cool. It does not mean that you have to agree to take them down to the piercing parlour and cheer them on; to do so would teach them nothing and would certainly not encourage them to develop a sense of cop on.

In this instance, your teenage child must understand that, just as you listened to their concerns, they must hear your concerns as you outline clearly why you do not feel this is the correct decision to make. Validation is a two-way process. But conversations of this nature can be somewhat open-ended; you could make an offer that when they are old enough to make a decision of that magnitude – say, 18 – *then* they can get the piercing done themselves, but that at this point in time they are unable to make that kind of a choice, so the decision lies with you. By doing so, you acknowledge that they may be upset with your decision, and that is not your intention, but that you are going to fulfil your responsibility as a parent and not permit the piercing at this time.

Squeaky-Wheel Syndrome

Another feature of visibility is what I like to refer to as 'Squeaky-Wheel Syndrome'. This refers to a dynamic in families where a troublesome sibling is the only one who appears to get attention. The difficult child becomes the 'squeaky wheel that gets the grease', which sends out the message to the other children that in order to be seen or validated they must be difficult, either by being troublesome (in the case of an externalising child) or by being withdrawn or unwell (in the case of an internalising child). This dynamic is very common in families, so it is important for parents to recognise it, as it is very easy to get into a situation where the independent or compliant child is left to their own devices because they don't 'need' help or intervention. This sometimes results in the independent child feeling lonely or invisible.

Validation and cop on

If a child can only be validated by success, then success will become overly important in their lives. This can have an impact from an early age, something I have seen first-hand many times throughout my career. Sometimes when I work with very young children, I offer a session during which I observe the parent playing with their child. This can seem artificial and not representative of real life at home, but I am often struck with how uncomfortable parents feel during the act of play. They much prefer to provide their small child with a toy that they can play with by themselves, which allows the parent to just observe. Play is a wonderful opportunity for early validation that is frequently missed. I will discuss this more under 'Involvement', the next element of the Therapeutic Milieu model. By playing with their child, a parent communicates their desire to spend time with their child. It also suggests to their child that playing time is of value to the parent. All of this is validating for the child; it makes them feel loved, and watched over and tells them that what's important to them (playing) is important to their parents too. Many parents observe their children in a playground, at a birthday party or on the sports field, but perhaps overlook the importance of joining in themselves.

Interestingly, the nature of the play itself is also important. While many electronic toys today do a great deal – move, fly, jump, beep, play music – research suggests that their appeal to children is short-lived. The more capable the toy, the more redundant the child is in interacting with it. Building blocks, dolls, action figures and creative toys are far more long-lasting, as they leave room for much more interaction and imagination. For example, a simple teddy can jump off the couch and wrestle dinosaurs, or build a city full of toys, or make dinner, whereas a spaceman sealed into a light-up flying spaceship clearly only goes to space – no imagination required. Toys that require more time and imagination to bring to life also allow parents to share a space for mutual learning with their children; a parent can help their child build either the prescribed contraption on the Lego box, or something else entirely that the child dreams up. In the process, they also build a relationship with their child that says, 'You are important, this is important and I value you.' This interaction can form the basis for a trajectory of closeness and mutual respect that continues for a long, long time.

How to play is a skill that we often lose over time. I regularly see a parent watch their child build a block tower, and, a few minutes into the task, the parent invariably takes over. A father might say something like, 'What about if you do it this way?' and his child will respond by becoming uninterested and moving on to something else. In this situation, it's important to remember that it does not matter if your child is building the block tower wrong; it is more important that you value playing with them and validate their attempt.

This is especially true with older children when it comes to sport, music and other activities in which children feel that getting it right is the only way to get attention and support from their parents – in other words, validation. Some children say that even though their parents go to every game they play, they still feel that they are not seen or heard. This can emerge when a child gets the feeling that their parent is there because they have to be or because they show no interest in talking about the game or sharing the experience with their child. This boils down to getting the balance of validation right: your child should feel validated, but not pressured.

> *Learning to validate your children's efforts is the most important thing you can do to improve communication with your children.*

All child mental health experts tell you that you need to have a good communicative relationship with your child, but they tend not to explain how you go about creating it. For me, learning to validate your children's efforts is the most important thing you can do to improve communication with your children. Teaching your children how to be open and honest communicators is, of course, to give them a wonderful attribute that they will take with them into adulthood.

If you take only one thing from this book, I hope it is this: never has validation from parents been more important for children than it is today. Ensuring that your children get real, face-to-face quality time at home, being acknowledged by people who love them, takes effort and hard work, but it is to my mind an investment of time that will pay you back ten times over in your children's ability to communicate and in their development of cop on.

Involvement

Last, but certainly not least, in the list of actions in the Therapeutic Milieu model is involvement. Involvement brings us right back to the theme of 'The less I'm heard, the more I shout', which is a concept that carries right through the model. Much of the childhood and adolescent behaviour that concerns parents comes from a feeling of not being heard, hence the emphasis in the 'how to' aspects of this book on the parent-child relationship and the communication styles that make this relationship more effective. So far, I have covered the importance of understanding your child during various phases of their development and looked at how best to nurture the parent-child relationship as they grow so you can encourage your children to make good decisions.

When it comes to learning how to make good decisions, children need to have some experience of good decisions being made with them and for them; in short, they need to know what a good decision looks like and how the decision-making process works.

When it comes to learning how to make good decisions, children need to have some experience of good decisions being made with them and for them; in short, they need to know what a good decision looks like and how the decision-making process works. An important way for children to gain this experience is by making the decisions about their own lives – this is how they can become 'involved'. This involvement, like so many of the elements of child-raising, needs to be paced correctly. Children should be involved in decisions in which they can and should have a voice and be spared from becoming overly involved in decisions that might overwhelm them or in topics that are beyond their stage of development or understanding.

Allowing children to be involved in some of the decisions that are made around aspects their lives, to a degree they can manage, is crucially important. Many young people say that they are not informed about decisions made by their parents that directly or indirectly affect them, and this can often lead to acting-out behaviours. This in some ways links back to visibility, in that the child feels that they are seen but perhaps not heard, and therefore must get their feelings across another way, which can lead to behavioural problems. This is understandable: no one likes decisions being made over their head without their input, and children and adolescents may act out in order to regain some control. A core aspect of child and adolescent development is this battle for control between child and parent, which begins as early as a toddler refusing to eat.

Some parents adopt the 'ignore it and it will go away' approach. However, if their child's core issue is that of not feeling involved, this will make the problem worse, by proving to the child that their feelings are not being taken into consideration again. Instead, you should contain the child's disgruntlement and involve them. This can be done in line with your child's stage of development and decision-making abilities. For example, a toddler who is refusing to eat could be involved in the preparation of their food, or their food could be made more appealing and less threatening by, say, your making mashed potato into animal shapes. A teenager who's angry about not being allowed to go to an over-18s disco could be involved in a plan to earn their parents' trust by adhering to successively later curfews to demonstrate their level of responsibility. Regardless of the scenario, giving your child a sense of involvement increases their sense of ownership and responsibility at a pace that they can manage and contributes greatly to the development of their cop on.

The illusion of control

As parents, it is important we draw on skills we've accumulated from all areas of our lives. I once met a businessman whose useful piece of advice has kept coming back to me: 'The best way to get staff on board with a new idea is to make them think it was their idea.' Initially, this seemed quite underhanded and sneaky to me, but when I gave it more thought it began to make much more sense. The struggle for power and autonomy is central to young people's interactions. Developing children are often ambivalent about the level of dependence they have on their parents, and so they like to see themselves as being in control. In most cases this is naïve, because they aren't ready to be in control, but that doesn't stop them from wanting it. Naturally, this is why books, movies and television shows in which a child is seen to outsmart their adult counterparts using wit and savvy, like Ben 10, Artemis Fowl and Harry Potter, appeal to children so much.

As a parent, you can use this fantasy of control to sow the seeds of new ideas in your children, allowing them to come around to your idea in their own time. Doing so allows your child to feel as if they're calling the shots but also gets the desired result for you.

For example, if you'd like a shy child to join a team sport they seem reluctant to try, you could build their confidence by encouraging them to play informally with their siblings, cousins or parents. You might bring them along to a training session to observe from afar, all the while suggesting encouragingly to them that they might enjoy it. This gentle sowing of seeds may mean that they choose to try it, and is different to nagging, which only serves to make children suspicious and resistant to taking part. It is crucial that this seed-sowing is done in line with your child's stage of development so as to support their growing independence at a rate that is not overwhelming. This gradual increasing of involvement in decision-making supports your child in becoming a good decision-maker and assists in the development of their skills of prioritising and self-awareness, and as a consequence it builds their sense of cop on.

Along similar lines, everyone prefers being 'asked' to do something rather than being 'told' to do it; it's all in the delivery. A request often creates a response based on a genuine desire to help out, whereas an order can create an angry or resentful response that results in whatever it is being done badly. Again, this makes sense: 'being asked' implies that you have some level of involvement in the outcome, that you have some control, whereas being told suggests that you are not to be involved in any related decision-making and, ultimately, that you have no control. The sense that you have a role or influence in something means that you give it more time, care and credence, and therefore you will do it better.

This can be obviously difficult when it comes to household chores like taking out the bins, but if we establish that a task has an end result that will be useful or pleasing to our children, we might get a better result. For example, in preparing to go to Granny's for the weekend, you could ask your toddler to help out by putting away her toys while you pack the bags. If she helps out by putting the toys in the box, you will all get to Granny's sooner, which is perhaps a better approach than 'If the playroom isn't clean, nobody will be going anywhere.' This notion of requesting a chore rather than demanding it can frame the whole principle of chipping in with household activities in a different light. It is best to start in with this kind of approach in the early years and re-establish it as your children get older. I am not saying that this will work every time, and of course children will resist boring tasks – as do we all – but perhaps this approach will improve your chances of success.

Involvement and cop on

If we include or involve our children in decisions, they will inevitably learn the processes that are incorporated into how we, as adults, make decisions. This involves informing our children as to how and why certain things happen and, where appropriate, asking them for their contributions. This process can occur even with the smallest child and becomes increasingly possible as our children become more sophisticated in their thinking.

The core aspect of cop on is the ability to weigh up the pros and cons of a situation and choose the sensible, measured and mature response. This ability, like most, must be taught over time, and we should lead by example to show our children this essential process in action. As with all the elements of the Therapeutic Milieu model, your child's involvement needs to be kept in line with the pace of their own development and they must only be involved in decisions that they can meaningfully understand. In cases where parents disagree about a decision, their child can sometimes become involved in disputes that ultimately do not concern them. Doing this overwhelms them more than it teaches them anything. A ten-year-old child involved in a conversation about her family's financial struggles might take away from the conversation that she is somehow to blame if the cost of her school books or the extracurricular activities come into question. She is old enough to understand that her activities cost money, and that some are a privilege, but isn't capable of understanding more. If parents are arguing over where they should go on a family holiday and put it to their 12-year-old to make the executive decision, this burdens their child with a sense of responsibility for the parents' happiness on holiday; giving the child a vote in the final decision might be better.

Equally, parents who do too much for their children, or who micro-manage their lives, prevent their children from having any role or voice in decisions. Ultimately, such children are being prevented from developing basic life skills. A parent who lays out their 12-year-old son's clothes, organises all his play dates or allows him to sleep with them in their bed is disabling their child's capacity to make appropriate decisions. More problematically, this also tells the child that their parent does not feel that he is able to make these decisions, which can diminish his self-esteem and create a vicious circle. As a result, when a time comes in his life where he has to make a decision, he won't know where to start. The sudden demand to work things out on his own may cause him to panic, as he hasn't become accustomed to having a role in their decisions so far. This ties in to the notion of 'killing someone with kindness'.

Parents might well imagine that offering their child any involvement in decisions gives the child too much power – and in some cases this is true. However, we know that with power comes responsibility, so if we want our children to learn to become gradually more responsible, we need to give them gradually more power, which involves increasing their levels of involvement in and power over their own lives.

Summary

In using Gunderson's five-element Therapeutic Milieu model – containment, structure, support, validation and involvement – as a framework for raising children, I am offering a simple, comprehensive approach that is flexible enough to handle almost everything that family life can throw at it. The model allows us to learn how to understand our children, bolster them, challenge them, hear them, include them and give them a structure to manage their concerns.

What is important to remember about this model is that the way in which the five elements apply to your child will vary according to the maturity, ability and life circumstance of the child. For example, a typical three-year-old will need more containment but less involvement, whereas a 17-year-old may need more involvement and less containment. The ebb and flow of these elements changes throughout your child's life, but the constant is a mindful parent, keeping an eye on what is most needed at each stage of your child's development.

Attention to all of these elements will teach your child to solve problems, develop cop on and, most importantly, develop an awareness of who they are and how they think and feel. If you pay attention to the fact that your child is a behavioural, thinking and emotional being, your child will learn to view themselves the same way. The better we know ourselves, the better we will be able to cope with our circumstances.

> *The ebb and flow of these elements changes throughout your child's life, but the constant is a mindful parent, keeping an eye on what is most needed at each stage of your child's development.*

Section Two

TECHNOLOGY AND FAMILY LIFE: bridging the generation gap and leading by example

THE TECHNOLOGICAL SEDUCTION

I was always very smug about my relationship with technology. I am adept at using my iPhone and computer, and I've always enjoyed all the little extras that having the world at your fingertips allows. Naturally, I was always of the opinion that I was far too sensible to lose myself to technology, to become dependent on it or to fall for the marketing ploys that suggest just how completely technology can and should rule your life. I chuckled at stories of internet addiction programmes being set up in the USA and China, and I was very much of the opinion that the people who supported these organisations had more money than sense. However, that all changed a couple of years ago when I experienced just how seductive technology can be first-hand, an experience that led me to pursue my doctoral research in this area.

'Mother and baby are well'

On 17 September 2012, my daughter was born. I decided to post a photo of her on Facebook alongside a brief status update that indicated the time she was born, what she weighed and the fact that both mother and baby were well. I posted this on my Facebook page because I figured it was easier than sending individual text messages to everybody. I hoped that during this very busy time I would be less likely to be bothered by numerous phone calls enquiring about how we all were; people could reply in texts or comments instead, which I could check *in my own time.*

Later that day, when I was on a trip back home to fetch some more supplies for my wife and daughter, I got a series of prompts by email to check my Facebook account, as I had received some responses to my earlier posting. I duly logged in, only to find that my post had received 27 likes and 14 comments. I was struck by this and felt quite happy and proud that my daughter had acquired such positive feedback. Feeling validated, I logged out and went about my business.

Later that evening I was prompted again to check Facebook. I now had 39 likes and an impressive 28 comments. I remember feeling that my wife must have given birth to the most beautiful baby in the world to have received such plentiful and positive feedback from all these people. Over the next day, I checked my Facebook page regularly for updates on the number of likes and comments that this beautiful photo – my daughter – had received. About two days later, the number of commenters and likers started to plateau, and it finished with an impressive 79 likes and 54 comments. 'Facebook fame has arrived', I thought, feeling quite smug about the whole experience. A day or two later I refreshed the page to see if there had been any stragglers with new likes or comments, but there were none. Nevertheless, I was delighted with the finishing result of 79 likes and 54 comments, all of which were complimentary and pleasant.

That was until two days later, when I realised that I actually had 142 Facebook friends, far more than the 79 who had commented on or liked my post. I wondered why people who had clearly been on Facebook since I had posted my photo, posting status updates and checking in to places, had not liked or commented on my baby daughter's photo or celebrated our good news. I remember feeling quite suspicious and a tad paranoid about these people. In a moment of madness, I wondered, 'Do these people not like my child?'

I realised I had been sucked in. I had become preoccupied with the validation that I enjoyed from the initial positive commentary from people, many of whom I would consider only acquaintances. 'As a man in his mid-thirties who has been through numerous years of personal therapy and would consider himself to be relatively well-adjusted, how did I let this happen to me?' I thought. I then considered how a similar situation would have played out if I were a 14-year-old, and how reliant on this feedback for validation and recognition I would have been. It got me thinking about the impact of social networking, technology and all kinds of computer-mediated communication on my life, and it triggered further considerations about similar phenomena in the context of my clinical work.

> *I always felt that my clinical experience would influence how I raised my children, and it certainly has. What I did not expect was the impact this experience would have in reverse: becoming a parent has given me new insight into my clinical work.*

I began to seriously consider the ever-changing dynamics within the landscape of contemporary communication and what they mean for our children and adolescents. I became a father for the first time in June 2010. I always felt that my clinical experience would influence how I raised my children, and it certainly has. What I did not expect was the impact this experience would have in reverse: becoming a parent has given me new insight into my clinical work. Being a child and adolescent psychotherapist and parent of young children can be both a blessing and a curse. My clinical work brings me very difficult cases, ranging from children with severe eating disorders and crippling anxiety problems to those suffering from severe depressive episodes and deliberate self-harm or even suicidal behaviour. It is an ongoing challenge not to view my own children's behaviour and my own parenting slip-ups through this lens. That is not to say that I feel I have this parenting thing all sorted or sussed – far from it: I struggle with it most days. However, my clinical work is a constant reminder of the possible consequences of my parenting pitfalls. As a result, I try to be constantly mindful of the stumbling blocks we all meet when raising children and to react quickly to them when they appear. I believe in the philosophy of the psychotherapist Isabel Menzies Lyth that it is better to contain failure than to fail to contain. My interpretation of this is accepting the fact that as parents we will fail; what is important is that we acknowledge each failure and attempt to manage them as best we can when they arise.

As a parent, one of the things I struggle to keep on top of the most is managing my relationship with technology. As in all things, I would like to be a good role model, showing my children how to have a reasonable, balanced relationship with technology and the online world. Regulation of our limitless access to technology and information is key. These days, technology is pervasive in our workplaces, our homes and our children's school and it has affected how we communicate, not only with our online connections but with our immediate family members and even ourselves.

This technological evolution should not be seen as all bad or all good. There are bound to be social casualties as we embrace such a massive movement that stands to impact on our relationships, our expectations and our lives. The rise of computer-mediated communication and internet technologies is simply the largest social experiment the world has ever witnessed, and, although it has not been around long enough for us to be aware of all its effects on our lives, here I will consider some of its most significant effects on our social world and, more specifically, on family life.

How we live and how we communicate

Like many people, I have a keen interest in technology. I try to keep abreast of most developing technologies and I am an active user of Facebook, Twitter and LinkedIn for both personal and professional purposes. I, like most people, regularly panic when I cannot access a Wifi signal or if I think that I have misplaced my phone. As a result, I know from personal experience how central technology is to our lives and how useful it is for work, play and keeping in touch.

In my work, however, I see a darker side to the omnipresence of technology in our lives. In response to these technological changes, the world of child and adolescent psychiatry has altered dramatically within the last ten years. Freud always suggested that in order to understand the normal we must investigate and understand the abnormal first. With this in mind, I believe that, although the psychological challenges that arise in my therapy room may exemplify the extremes of what is happening in the mainstream population, we would do well to consider them and to reflect on where we all sit on the spectrum of relationships with technology.

Concerns that were not a feature of our services ten years ago include such things as cyberbullying, online and offline gaming addiction, social network addiction, problematic relationships with online pornography, online sexualisation and encounters with online sexual predators. Naturally, problems of dependency, addiction and unhealthy relationships existed long before the internet, but these specific difficulties are new terms in the discourse of mental health. More importantly, they are presenting with an altogether eerie regularity. Due to the unregulated, instantaneous, worldwide and potentially public nature of online communication, these types of difficulties now have more sinister, far-reaching consequences than their pre-online forms. The magnitude of these consequences means that, although the problems are not altogether different, their impact most certainly can be.

Problems of dependency, addiction and unhealthy relationships existed long before the internet, but … due to the unregulated, instantaneous, worldwide and potentially public nature of online communication, these types of difficulties now have more sinister, far-reaching consequences than their pre-online forms. The magnitude of these consequences means that, although the problems are not altogether different, their impact most certainly can be.

These problems are but one part of the changes in how young people communicate these days and of the impact technology has on their developmental trajectory. These issues have created a culture that is significantly different from what I knew as a teenager. In saying this, I don't mean to lament youth culture of days gone by nor do I want to come across as an alarmist about the dangers of technological advancement. Rather, I want to highlight some of the changes that have occurred in all of our lives and illustrate the new developmental challenges that are part and parcel of these changes for young people.

In this section of the book, I will explore our new social context and the challenges it has brought, pointing out what is gained and what gets lost as society changes, how these gaps affect our children and our parenting styles, and what we can do to correct the balance. In the last section, I will provide some helpful and hopeful advice about improving our children's self-esteem, managing their anxieties and increasing their resilience.

The 'on demand' culture

I borrow the term 'on demand' from the marketers of my wonderful digital TV recorder – it's both 'always on' and 'on demand'. It's a common enough device and another example of how technology can make our lives easier. You can pre-record and save your favourite TV shows, sparing you a suspense-filled week of waiting to find out the answer to the latest 'whodunnit', or download your whole favourite series instantly online, all in one go. The best part is that you can fast-forward through the ads or the credits or anything you don't fancy. Like a lot of people, I rarely ever watch television in 'real time'. As a busy parent, professional, student and now author, I use my wonderful digital TV recorder to record my favourite programmes and watch them, usually at some ungodly hour, when I have time to do so.

Occasionally, though, I manage to watch something live, usually something topical. One such recent exception was the World Cup. During a key match I recall growing genuinely frustrated that I had to sit through the ads at the half-time break. I was so used to being able to press a button to fast-forward these inconvenient thieves of my time that, when I couldn't, I lost the plot. I had developed a dependency on my Sky Plus device. 'Cop on, Colman,' I thought. This was the very definition of a 'First World problem' – but I wasn't the only person in the house who had it. I recently recorded a children's movie for my four-year-old, a film that happened to be on one of the terrestrial TV stations. This meant it too was interrupted by advertisements, which led my son to come running into the kitchen to inform me that our TV was 'broken', as the movie had been interrupted. Both of these examples illustrated for me my family's dependence on the digital TV recorder and the low tolerance for interruption this device brought into our home.

With the advent of recordable television, we have lost the paradoxical pleasure of waiting for the next instalment, which used to be how many kinds of entertainment were marketed; this is no longer even a feature of our world. Now, whole series are marketed once they are released online for binge-watching. I have already looked at how learning to wait brings significant rewards. I see this on-demand culture as reaching well beyond our TV and broadband providers; it's indicative of how we look at life and how we think. In the on-demand culture there is no time to wait; everything should be accessible instantaneously. It's hard to argue with the appeal of recordable television, or fast-acting pain relief, or knowing when the next bus is coming; however, although the on-demand culture appears to make everything easier, it also artificially creates demands on us that make things much harder.

Let's go back to my experience of watching the World Cup game in real time. I became indignant at the prospect of waiting for three minutes while a series of ads played. This irritation came from my sense of what is and is not acceptable. The acceptability of something is understood in context, and as the on-demand culture develops and things become easier to access, our expectations are consequently increased. The on-demand culture increases our level of demand and lowers our capacity for patience.

One of the most problematic aspects of the on-demand culture for young people today is the promise of entertainment on demand. I remember a colleague asking me when I purchased my first iPhone, 'Are you not worried you'll never be bored again?' I interpreted this as a mark of my colleague's jealousy, but, on reflection, he was making a really valid point. In a world where you can get whatever you want on demand, there is no space for boredom – or waiting, or patience. We expect every moment to be filled with activity, and if it is not we always have an online device to hand to entertain ourselves. You can see this anywhere and everywhere, in any situation where there is a gap in an activity. The next time you are standing in a queue at the supermarket, take a moment and look around. The rest of the queue will be reaching for, typing into or checking something on their smartphones. The majority of people will be looking down. Crucially, this shows how technology is shaping our interactions with those around us. Where previously we might have given a friendly glance to the person in the queue behind us, passed the time of day or made small talk with another human being, we're now checking email and Facebook or sending a text. Every doctor's waiting room is the same. As a culture, it is apparent that we now do not have to just wait, so our skill at waiting is becoming less developed.

As a 'digital immigrant', a term I'll explain in more detail later, you developed your waiting skills in your pre-internet life; although, like me, you may have forgotten how to use them, you know that you can if you really have to. Learning to wait is a considerable developmental task that everyone needs to master, as it leads to an ability to delay gratification and cope with stress. Our capacity to delay gratification and tolerate frustration is a core indicator for our later success in life, as the famous Stanford 'marshmallow experiment' proved. The marshmallow experiment is a famous study carried out through the late '60s and early '70s by Professor Walter Mischel. The study examined children's capacity for delayed gratification by offering them the simple choice of one marshmallow that they could eat straight away, or two marshmallows if they could resist eating the first marshmallow for 15 minutes. The children were left unsupervised in a room with the marshmallow so that their capacity for delayed gratification could be assessed. The findings of a series of follow-up studies revealed that those children who waited generally did better in life than those who did not. They had better exam scores and lower body mass indexes and went further in their education. The study illustrates how an early capacity for decision-making by problem-solving and contextualising can be a positive indicator for broader success in later life. The capacity to contextualise and reframe our experiences and to use our reason, knowing that we can survive surmountable stress, are core indicators of resilient and robust mental health.

Children today lack the pre-technological experience of having to learn to wait without constant entertainment, and as a consequence may struggle with having to tolerate frustration. It is worth noting that we as parents often use the expression 'learn to wait', implying that we see this task as something worth putting some effort into achieving. This also suggests that waiting is not an innate skill but an ability that has to be acquired. With the on-demand culture as their benchmark, our children's high expectations of the world are regularly met and their capacity to tolerate frustration is limited.

> *With the on-demand culture as their benchmark, our children's high expectations of the world are regularly met and their capacity to tolerate frustration is limited.*

'It would be better if it moved'

With the move towards Web 2.0 (the name given to the progressive humanisation of technology, discussed in more detail at the end of this section) and the increased interactivity between technology and human emotion, the effects on our expectations, values and tolerance are clear. Quick and easy access to all information, our ability to Google something instead of working it out and the improvements in technological realism are changing what we value. The psychoanalyst and MIT researcher Sherry Turkle describes a story one of her research participants told her, about a group of school children taken to a world-famous museum on their school trip. In the foyer they were met by a ginormous set of dinosaur bones reconstructed into a skeleton in order to illustrate the size of the beast and its sheer magnitude. The museum guide proceeded to tell the group with great enthusiasm about the history of this remarkable species, its attributes in life, and the time and effort that went into excavating the fossils and creating the display. As the group moved on, the teacher asked what the children thought, expecting them to be in awe. The group's response was 'It would have been better if it moved – or roared.' This group judged the value of this experience not on the meaning of the story behind the structure or the richness of the tale of the dinosaur's life and its discovery after death. Instead, the group was so accustomed to interactive technology that they held the real (and, in this case, prehistoric) world to the same standards. To this group, the authenticity of the dinosaur was less important than its ability to interact with them. So when the technological bar is raised, our real-life expectations rise in accordance with it.

In recent years, I have spoken with a number of young people who feel low or anxious about growing up, worrying about their future lives. I am struck by the levels of expectation that some of these young people have of life. When they look at their future in terms of finishing their Leaving Certificate, going to college, getting a job, maybe getting married and having children, they don't consider that to be a desirable life. 'Where is the fun in that?' they ask. Instead of the standard life plans common to so many of us, some young people are weighed down by the expectation that they need to 'make their mark on the world' and do something 'extraordinary'. They don't just want a one-of-a-kind dinosaur skeleton – they want it to move.

DIGITAL IMMIGRANTS AND DIGITAL NATIVES

The terms 'digital immigrant' and 'digital native' were coined by the writer and games designer Marc Prensky in 2001 to describe the two groups of people who now have relationships with the internet and technology. He defines digital immigrants as people who, like me, knew a world before the internet; we had to migrate into an online world. In Ireland, the world of the internet began in the late '90s and became more mainstream in the early 2000s. So those of us who were adults or were approaching adulthood at this time can be considered digital immigrants.

Young people who were born just before, during or after this period have no experience of a pre-internet world and so are considered digital natives; the online world is their world, and always has been. It is sometimes hard to believe that the internet and its technological counterpart, the mobile phone, are so young and have only been a feature of our lives for such a short time. I remember sitting in St Ita's in Portrane in 1998 as a postgraduate student nurse with a classmate of mine who was trying to explain to me the concept of texting. 'Why don't you just phone them and have the conversation? That will never take off,' I responded. How wrong was I?

It is certainly not the case that digital immigrants are clueless when it comes to technology, as many older people are incredibly technologically able. The main difference between digital natives and digital immigrants is in how they form relationships, both with the online world and with each other. A digital immigrant can contextualise their online interactions with reference to their pre-internet world. This offers them a 'grounding' that allows them to be a critical consumer of technology. A digital native has no such reference point; it is as if the digital native has arrived into the world in the middle of a conversation. It is the responsibility of the digital immigrant to fill them in on what has gone before so that they too can enjoy the benefits of context, which gives them a sense of relative value or meaning. Without context, digital natives risk understanding only half the story.

> *It is as if the digital native has arrived into the world in the middle of a conversation. It is the responsibility of the digital immigrant to fill them in on what has gone before.*

Digital immigrants remember having to go to the chemist to get their photos developed; they went to a travel agent to book a flight; and they wrote letters and posted them to people who lived far away in order to communicate with them. Digital natives, on the other hand, are happy to do almost everything online – and do. In discussing how the challenges of contemporary society may differ for the digital immigrant and the digital native, the goal is to better understand the thinking of young people and to begin to bridge the gap between our contrasting experiences by exploring how one can complement the other. We live in a pre-figurative society, which means that, given the advancements of the technological evolution, the young are teaching the older generation for the first time. This role reversal is not only about our children teaching us about their online world; the flip-side is that we as parents need to teach our children about the offline world, in order to instil in them the values that were and are still deeply important in society and relationships. The move towards online convenience, speed and easy access is a change for the better, but it is not perfect.

Where aspects of children's development are concerned, parents should be aware that some things are falling through the cracks.

> *We live in a pre-figurative society, which means that ... the young are teaching the older generation ... This role reversal is not only about our children teaching us about their online world; the flip-side is that we as parents need to teach our children about the offline world, in order to instil in them the values that were and are still deeply important in society and relationships.*

A few years ago, American researchers assessed the skills and abilities of a large group of two- to five-year-olds. Almost all the children could operate a computer mouse; a high percentage of them could complete a computer game from start to finish; and an even higher percentage could navigate and browse the internet. However, of the sample surveyed, almost 89 per cent could not tie their shoelaces, and 48 per cent could not ride a bike. Along similar lines, a colleague who is a public health nurse suggested to me that there is some discussion in developmental clinics for very young children that digital developmental tasks are replacing traditional 'building blocks' tasks, as many children now seem more adept at swiping screens than lifting and placing blocks. It is up to us as parents to ensure that, where children gain new skills, they don't lose the more traditional ones, so as not to compromise our children's social and functional development. The need to nurture and encourage sense, sensibility, maturity, resilience and cop on is all the more important when there is so much emphasis on developing digital and technological skills.

While digital immigrants often expect digital natives to be able to identify the futility or flaws inherent in technology and its uses, we can sometimes forget that a computer-filled existence is their only reality. So while they can manipulate the technology itself with ease, they may struggle with the psychological, emotional or social savvy required for interacting with the *people* on the other end of the technology. Honestly, every week in my therapy room I have a conversation in which parents (digital immigrants) are becoming frustrated by their adolescent children (digital natives) for their lack of cop on in their dealings with people, either online or in person.

But this lack of cop on is in part due to the nature of the technologies that young people use to communicate, as they both limit how much we can say and shape the way we say it. Text messages, for example, restrict us to only a limited number of (often abbreviated) words, finished occasionally with an accompanying icon indicating our intended emotion. Texting is of course an effective way of communicating information in a succinct manner that saves time compared with a phone call. Of course, the flip-side of this is that we now communicate far more by means of the typed word than face-to-face, so we lose the often essential information that can be gained from the body language, facial expressions or tone of voice that a personal or phone encounter would provide to varying degrees. Irish people in particular have embraced texting to a startling degree. The European statistics-compiling body EUROSTAT revealed in 2012 that Ireland was among the highest-ranking countries when it came to texting – sending 2,700 messages per inhabitant in 2009. (Ireland also recorded 119 mobile phone contracts per 100 persons.) The psychologist and author of *Body Language*, James Borg, contends that only 7 per cent of communication is based on words themselves – so a text message misses 93 per cent of what is being communicated. As digital immigrants, we (in theory) learned to communicate during our pre-internet lives; digital natives did not, instead learning all their verbal and physical communication skills *at the same time* as learning to communicate with technology. Inevitably, communicating with technology influences how digital natives communicate more generally. This, I think, is reason enough to explore the attraction of this form of communication for young people, in addition to examining the strengths and weaknesses of this way of relating.

> *As digital immigrants, we (in theory) learned to communicate during our pre-internet lives; digital natives did not, instead learning all their verbal and physical communication skills* at the same time *as learning to communicate with technology.*

iPhone envy: the infant attachment process

One of the core elements of early child development is the attachment process that occurs between an infant and their primary caregivers, typically their parents. Within the attachment process there is a natural dynamic that involves children competing for the attention of their primary caregiver, be it competition with their siblings, the other parent or even visitors to the family home. This is an apparently simple but often complex dynamic that involves children managing their anxiety about parental abandonment by trying to hold their parents' attention and

maintain their own visibility. Many young children engage
in problematic attachment behaviours that are very familiar
to parents: panic when a parent exits the room, leaves them
with a babysitter or tries to get them to start school. Most
of these attachment problems improve with time without
any intervention when children learn that their parents will
'hold them in mind' even when they are not there, so the
separation anxiety reduces.

Nowadays, there is a new focus for parental attention with
which children must compete for attention and visibility:
technology. Now children not only have to contend with
other family members and occasional visitors for their
parents' attention at home: they must also compete with
a device that is rarely out of their parents' grasp or line of
vision. Psychoanalysis places a great deal of emphasis on
the power of the gaze – what it means to look at another
person and to be looked at. As noted when considering the
idea of containment, this is particularly true in the mother-
child relationship, particularly when the mother 'holds the
child in her gaze', which illustrates the 'containing' influence
of being looked at and so almost 'looked after'. For children
looking on and competing for their parents' attention, the
captivating, entrancing quality of a smartphone or tablet
makes it an object of intense desire, interest and mystique.
Clearly, in this scenario we are showing our children that our
relationship with technology is of grave importance to us,
one to be envied – and envy they do, from a very early age.

The seductive nature of technology and the insidious
way it has woven itself into our lives is such that we often
find ourselves transfixed or preoccupied by it, sometimes
without our noticing. This kind of passive reliance creates

a dependence on our smartphone – no longer merely a phone with which to make and receive calls and texts, but an electronic diary with our personal photos, emails, calendars, contacts, to-do lists and other important personal records. The smartphone is our digital hub and the journal of our existence; of course it attracts our gaze. They're attractive, small, lit-up devices with which we appear to share an emotional connection: when we look at it, it sometimes makes us happy and sometimes sad. Whatever the relationship, it's clearly an important one, as we carry it around with us everywhere we go and we constantly check that we have not lost it. If I were an infant, I would certainly feel I needed to compete with that.

Multi-tasking or rudeness?

Wherever we are these days and whoever we're with, we tend to be doing more than one thing at a time. It is no longer enough to be minding a child, sitting on a train, watching television, buying something in a shop or talking to a friend; we now do all that and more while interacting with someone else, somewhere else, with our mobile phone, tablet or computer, at the same time.

'Multi-tasking' has been in vogue in recent years and we are frequently told that this capability is a real skill. Only a few years ago, the idea that we could be talking to a friend and see them check their hand-held device mid-conversation for an update on Facebook, a tweet, a text or an email would have been unthinkable; it would have been seen as rude in the past, but I am not sure that this is still the case. Many of my adolescent clients leave their smartphones face up on the arm of their chairs in my rooms and I notice them glancing towards the screen regularly throughout their sessions. This could be a comment on the boring nature of my therapeutic conversations, but I believe it is part of a broader cultural norm.

In a host of situations, it now seems to be accepted that multiple stimuli, technological or otherwise, should be used at the same time. In some fields, it seems to be perfectly acceptable to take your laptop into a work meeting and be completing your work whilst the meeting is going on. This illustrates the idea that people now attend meetings (i.e. take the time to sit down and interact with their colleagues face-to-face) only for the aspect of the meeting directly relevant to them and their work; they look up and engage for this part, but otherwise they appear to be psychologically elsewhere. This is an example of avoiding conversation, editing your availability to others and displaying your fear of missing out on something important elsewhere – albeit a fear of missing out on only what *you* consider to be most important.

An organisation that functions in this way can struggle to create a culture of collegiality and interpersonal support among its employees. An increased emphasis on the capacity to work alone might mean employees fail to develop working relationships, or that their work is more about tasks and less about people. The corporate world pays lip service to the importance of teamwork and connectedness, yet common workplace phrases like 'I have to get rid of a few emails' or 'I spent an hour this morning trudging through emails' suggest otherwise – that connecting with people is a hassle. Perhaps the humanisation of technology is dehumanising our communications. Email, in-house instant messaging, texts and conference calls give the sender little sense of how the recipient is responding to the communication – where's the 'connectedness' in that? If we are not reminded of how our communications affect other people, we run the risk of becoming immune to interpersonal sensitivities, diluting our emotional intelligence and chipping away at our sense of working in a team.

> *If we are not reminded of how our communications affect other people, we run the risk of becoming immune to interpersonal sensitivities, diluting our emotional intelligence and chipping away at our sense of working in a team.*

This new way of relating – or perhaps not relating – is not confined to business scenarios; notably, it has permeated our social lives too. I am sure we can all relate to the frustration of putting time aside to go to meet with friends in the local pub for a chat only to find that they spend half the time they're with you communicating with someone else, somewhere else. Needless to say, this is a deeply invalidating experience.

'I'd rather text than call'

The internet and online technologies are supposed to save us time – that's how they're sold. The same is true for the globalisation and the mobilisation of the workforce through advances in information technology. Initially, we thought that 'If I can bang off an email, it will save me having to call.' For digital immigrants, this is applied most frequently in the world of business. However, the young people I meet on a daily basis use the same approach in their personal lives; they would rather make – or receive – a text than a call, even among their closest friends. The psychoanalyst Sherry Turkle describes how these modern forms of communication are designed to avoid the 'messiness of conversation'. The messiness of conversation refers to the everyday pleasantries that tend to accompany a phone call; with text and emails, we can now communicate with the bare minimum of what we need to say and can do away with all that 'packaging'. We can edit, cut and delete aspects of how we relate to each other, trimming away the fat of conversation – anything that is uninteresting or surplus to requirements – leaving just the lean cut of information.

Often, however, when a conversation is edited down to just the absolutely necessary, the time we had hoped to save gets invested in the preparation of the email, rather than an actual conversation. My young clients describe spending hours creating the perfect status update or the perfect response to a message from a potential girlfriend or boyfriend. Again, most of us adults can relate; we routinely commit far too much time to composing an important email, reading and re-reading the latest draft to make sure it's just right before we send it. This isn't even to mention the huge numbers of emails we all now receive and how they build up, unanswered, costing us all time.

Beyond the time-saving myth of email, there's its omnipresence. Where once work correspondence was handled during working hours, we now have work emails on our smartphones 24/7. So, in addition to spending lots of time writing emails, we're expected to be constantly accessible by email. As much as this mobilises our workspace and in theory permits us some flexibility in our schedules, it also intrudes upon our non-work space: family life. Colleagues think twice about phoning you while you are on a family holiday in Dingle, but they don't hesitate to send off an email, knowing that you may well check your phone, despite being on holiday, and perhaps feel obliged to respond.

Our edited selves online

The level of control we exert over how we relate to other people extends to how we 'edit' ourselves online, presenting a carefully curated picture of who we are. Nowhere is this truer than in the more intimate aspects of our lives online, such as meeting a potential life partner. The meteoric rise in popularity of internet dating sites demonstrates Sherry Turkle's theory about avoiding the messiness of communication, and it clearly illustrates how dramatically the way we connect with each other has changed. Dating sites allow their users to whittle down a list of their prospective suitors by reviewing their profiles. Online dating profiles are merely a snapshot of who we are and, needless to say, demand that we put our best foot forward, meaning that users reveal only selected positive aspects of themselves. The 'messiness' of making a bad first impression is reduced, as we're allowed to read over what we are about to say before we post it. Ultimately, we post an edited version of ourselves here and on Facebook, Twitter, LinkedIn and any of the social networking sites we use for work or play.

The trouble with this, particularly for the digital native, is that it perpetuates the illusion that everyone can be perfect. Yet it is in the very messiness of communication that we reveal our true selves; we are tested by our ability to relate to other people and, in those tests, we grow up. Anyone who has had a romantic relationship will know that it is often the acceptance of another's flaws that allows a relationship to be sustained over time, rather than an appreciation of their positive qualities. Conversations, like relationships, *are* messy. They need to be in order to be real.

The online world offers relationships that aren't founded on reality – and relationships that don't exist in reality. They come with a level of control that simply doesn't exist in the real world, as a conversation or flow of information can be turned off, ignored or otherwise manipulated without the immediate consequences such behaviour might create in real time. As much as I might like to, I cannot switch my settings to 'offline' when my wife wants me to bring out the bins while I am watching an important rugby game. I can't be offline when she comes home after a hard day at work and wants to give out. Thankfully, she couldn't be offline when I needed her support when I had writer's block in writing this book. Relationships are not conditional on circumstances being within our control and, most importantly, relationships are not neat, they're messy. It is in the midst of this messiness that real relationships are discovered and developed.

————

The above examples of this always-accessible, always-available culture apply to members of the workforce, whom we can assume are well-adjusted adults and digital immigrants. Clearly, we have all been seduced to some degree into this new way of relating and being that intrudes so significantly into our everyday lives. Consider then young digital natives, who are being integrated into this world; they too are being taught that 24/7 accessibility is a requirement of life today. Even more so than their adult counterparts, they can struggle to manage this demanding way of life – and they need our help.

CHILDREN IN INTERNET CITY

The actor and self-professed technology addict Stephen Fry famously suggested that, in order to understand the internet, we must see it as a city.

> It's got all these nice, safe cycle paths and child-friendly parks and all the rest of it … and, like any great city, it has monumental libraries and theatres and museums and places in which you can learn and pick up information, and there are facilities for you that are astounding – specialised museums, not just general ones.
>
> But there are also slums and there are red light districts and there are really sleazy areas where you wouldn't want your children wandering alone.
>
> And you say, 'But how do I know which shops are selling good gear in the city and how do I know which are bad? How do I know which streets are safe and how do I know which aren't?' Well, you find out.

That's just it: as parents, we have to find out whether our child's route to school passes through a bad neighbourhood and we have to prepare them for it. The internet is no different: the responsibility of learning what our children might encounter and of teaching them what to do is ours. Sometimes parents claim to be technologically unable or technologically uninterested, but this effectively means sending their child out into a city with no supervision or guidance.

Recently I travelled to London to present at an international conference about whether internet use by young patients in in-patient and residential mental health settings should be permitted. My argument was that it should, as I believe prohibition prevents young people from developing the ability to manage and negotiate the internet, an omnipresent technology which is and will continue to be a significant part of their lives. A debate ensued, but I maintained my position: internet access is not problematic if there are supports in place to promote sense and sensibility in the user.

When constructing this argument, I considered my own trip to London that day, drawing parallels between how I had prepared for the trip and how we should prepare young people for 'travelling' on the internet. Before I left, my mother advised me to 'watch out on that Underground Tube', as she had heard that it was a favourite spot of pick-pockets. She told me to spread my money in different pockets and to keep my passport and tickets in a zipped pocket. She reminded me to check the routes to and from the conference and the airport before I left and to leave myself plenty of time. I humoured my mother by listening as she imparted all this advice and as I thought, 'I am a man in my mid-thirties travelling to London, where I once lived for over two years.' I was well aware of the dangers of the city and had my own plans on how I would manage them. Yet on the Tube that day, a rather suspicious man was acting oddly on my carriage and I found myself moving my money around my pockets and putting my passport into my jacket pocket, which was zipped. Despite all my assumed knowledge and experience, when I became unnerved it was my mother's advice that I remembered and acted upon.

I believe that our relationships with our children about their use of technology need to be quite similar. We need to teach our children to navigate this space as we would encourage them to negotiate a large city and to provide them with all the resources available to help them. Children need to be aware of the dangers they may encounter and the wrong turns they may take and of how to get help if they find themselves down a street where they know they should not be.

Understanding our children's online worlds

One thing about childhood is that it is universal; we have all been there, so we should all be able to remember it. But you would be surprised how quickly we selectively forget aspects of our childhood when we are expected to empathise with our own children's experiences. In order to negotiate being a parent, we must first learn to understand the environment in which our children live. Some aspects of childhood today will be much like our own, while others will be entirely new or experienced in new ways. Learning more about our children's situation is crucial to understanding how they experience and function in their world. With an insight into the world of digital natives, we as parents can better form a meaningful connection with our children in order to foster good, open lines of communication. The teenage complaint that their parents 'don't know what it's like' is not new, but perhaps given the monumental advancements and changes that have occurred in recent years it is all the more relevant.

As with all attempts to relate to other people's situations, sometimes a little bit of effort is all it takes to open these lines of communication. Parents need to learn enough about their children's worlds and how they work so that their children will feel able to approach them with any questions or concerns they may have. This communication should include more than just their online worlds; you should keep up to date about changes in your child's social circles, the ethos and environment of their school, and their extracurricular activities.

Most recent failures to try to understand each other across the generations often occur over children's use of technology. Faced with a child whose head is always stuck in their phone, parents often get frustrated, and a battle of wills ensues. Unfortunately, this response only serves to make their child feel misunderstood, causing them to talk to their parents even less and retreat further into their phones, whereas their peers are less judgemental and understand them better. While attempts to take away or limit your child's use of their phone force the child to engage with you, you can more often than not be left with a grumpy, resentful child who feels that you have disconnected them from their world. Attempts by parents to replace their children's phone time with other activities only work when the activities are actually things their children enjoy – rather than what the parents think they should enjoy.

Parents need to step back to try to understand the draw of social media from their children's perspective and the enormity and intensity of young people's relationships with their friends both on and off line. Parents must accept that, no matter what they think of their children's online world, playing down the dramas of childhood in the schoolyard, on the football pitch, on Facebook or with a new romance conducted mainly by text isn't helpful.

It is not easy for parents to learn about or become involved in supervising their children's internet access, particularly as many young people see cyberspace very much as a 'parent-free zone'; recent migrations of young people from Facebook to Twitter were due in part to their parents opening Facebook accounts and wanting to be 'friends' with their children. My advice to parents has always been that supervision, or rather a lack of supervision, is a process that is earned rather than given. You can begin with tight supervision of your child's online activities but gradually give them more space and privacy on the internet as appropriate, just as you would with any kind of freedom – walking to the local shop or to a friend's house and then graduating to taking the bus into town, for example. Like all freedoms, it should be earned relative to the amount of cop on your child has demonstrated over time.

The virtual community

Beyond the world of technology, there have been many other changes in Ireland in the last decade with regard to how we relate to each other and live our lives. The most obvious has been the arrival and departure of the Celtic Tiger. The property boom that fuelled it changed the way we thought about and spoke about our homes, our lives and our money. We had a larger amount of disposable income, and for the period from 1999 to 2008 the economic landscape in Ireland looked good.

There were many knock-on effects of all this change for Irish society, not least in the ways that families functioned.

These changes were not the same for everybody, of course, but in the main the Celtic Tiger shifted our sense of community. During the Celtic Tiger, I began to hear young people, and some older people, reporting a new kind of disconnect from each other. From my pre-Celtic Tiger experience I remembered families who reported a sense of familial and community support they depended upon in times of need. Communities used to respond to a local bereavement; they circled the wagons and reached out to help one another. Although this sense of community is often associated with a rural setting, it was seen in more urban communities too.

But with the Celtic Tiger, this connection with community began to ebb away. Families living in cramped new housing estates or apartment blocks did not have a strong sense of community. What became clear to me was that, outside school, most children's social networks were established in organised extracurricular activities. Naturally, parents made an effort to ensure their children got to know other children in their area through whatever activities were on offer, but the volume and intensity of these activities soon verged on the extreme. It appeared that the absence of a local community network was compensated for with many different activities for each child at one time, such as scouts, ballet, football, guitar lessons, drama classes and karate. Suddenly, children were engaged in so many activities that they had little or no time to establish a social network that hadn't been structured for them – in other words, to find their own friends in their area. Some theorists suggest that the absence of a local community is the very reason young people are forced to create online social networks and communities: to compensate.

Another major societal change that has an impact on young people's lives today is the recent focus on child safety. Many of us shudder to imagine our children doing nowadays what we did as children, because of our heightened awareness of children's safety and the dangers that seem to abound. I walked home from primary school on a country road when I was a child, thumbing a lift home from every car that passed. Naturally, there is no way I would permit my children to do anything like that now, and I think I am absolutely right to have that view. These days, our anxiety about our children's safety demands that someone supervise our children at all times. As a result, many young people spend much more time at home, indoors – where they can be watched easily. Unsurprisingly, the more time they spend indoors, without their friends, the more time they spend online with them.

Recent psychological research by Danah Boyd (2014) in the USA suggests that we have driven our children online by making their offline worlds so sterile and uninteresting, so afraid are we that they might get hurt in the real world. We have become so anxious about child safety that we do not permit children to run in school playgrounds, or teenagers to congregate in school yards after school hours. Consequently, there is nowhere available for them to explore their identities or even to just 'hang out'. It is no wonder they migrate onto social networks for a bit of privacy and free time when they get home. As is often the case, the parent downstairs makes the mistake of confusing 'presence' with 'safety', thinking, 'As long as I know my child is upstairs in his room on his computer, I know he is safe'. Stepping back, however, we can see that if he is accessing a portal to the virtual world, this could be the furthest thing from the truth.

In part as a result of this, we are witnessing an undeniable increase in online communities, best described as 'virtual tribes'. As with any tribe, virtual tribes gather and connect regularly online, which encourages members to behave in similar ways and communicate using similar means and codes. This behaviour can encourage meaningful connections between members and can often also encourage a 'group think' mentality, which will be discussed later in this section. A virtual community is made up of a network of people often linked by weak ties – people who don't have close relationships with each other. For young people, 'hanging out' in communities of their peers (be it in person or online) is much more important developmentally than can be objectively observed. It is through hanging out with peers that we explore intimate relationships, develop our identities and establish a sense of ourselves; if young people spend much of this formative time in regular contact with people they don't know well, it can stand to influence them more than perhaps it should. Every young person needs to individuate from their parents, a process that involves making decisions, problem-solving, experimentation and building social skills. Traditionally, this was negotiated through a close network of usually six to ten close friends. An online social network, however, is much larger, meaning that the audience for this experimentation is not as well known to young people, not as intimate and perhaps not as 'friendly' in the true sense, meaning they are open to higher degrees of critical feedback.

Interestingly, research suggests that the maximum number of actual friends that someone can feasibly have is 150, known as the 'Dunbar number'. My young clients sometimes have upwards of 1,000 Facebook friends. This number itself often becomes an issue, as it is seen as a social-status rating by which young people can be judged. A young person once told me that 400 Facebook friends was respectable, 900 was impressive, but 150 was 'just sad'.

So what is the knock-on effect of this kind of hanging out? If these large virtual networks hold social currency, how does this affect young people's ability to relate to other people, and how in turn does this alter their development, identity and sense of themselves? One of the major developments born of our always-on culture is the fear of missing out – understandable if you're expected to keep on top of developments and intrigue with hundreds of 'friends' online.

FOMO: FEAR OF MISSING OUT

'Fear of Missing Out' has been described as a modern syndrome for our communication-obsessed age, a fear that encroaches on many aspects of our lives (Claire Cohen, *Daily Telegraph*, 16 May 2013). In my therapy room, I have heard of young people who set alarms on their phones to wake them throughout the night so they can check social networking sites to make sure they are not missing out on anything. This inability to regulate themselves applies equally to other online activities, such as gaming, which is suspected to have quite addictive qualities. I have encountered parents who have been up at 4 a.m. to unplug fuses in order to stop their children playing online games like 'Call of Duty' or 'Grand Theft Auto'. Others have described having to come back from their family holiday abroad because there was no Wifi available and their children became unmanageable as a result of their FOMO. These extreme forms of being always accessible are signs of poor regulation, a difficulty that is common to many aspects of adolescent life but one that parents and children can work to manage – with a little cop on. I will consider here the different ways that FOMO can be seen at work with young people on social media and how it can shape their views and actions.

Group think

'Group think' is a force frequently at work among adolescents. As young people strive to define their identity, they often take on the views of their peer group rather than forming their own opinions, values and beliefs. In this way, peer pressure plays a significant role in the decision-making process during this life stage.

Traditionally, the power of adolescent group think was challenged by familial influences, which often added a bit of perspective. I remember my sister coming home one evening after school and declaring she was now a vegetarian because her friend Elaine (who happened to be quite cool and had some social status in the group) did not think that eating animals was right. My sister's indignation took us all by surprise, and that evening she scowled at the rest of us as we tucked in to our Findus Chicken Crispy Pancakes. The following day my mother prepared my sister's favourite dinner, spaghetti Bolognese, for the rest of us and made her a rather vile-looking lentil stew. My sister was not overly keen on the stew and managed about four forkfuls. My mother left out a particularly delicious-looking plate of Bolognese on the countertop for the rest of the evening. At 10 p.m. my mother appeared looking quite smug and I saw through the crack in the kitchen door my sister, tucking in to the Bolognese. She was no longer a vegetarian. My mother's strategy was not particularly anti-vegetarian, nor under other circumstances would she have been so sneaky. But she spotted that my sister's choice was based on someone else's value system, not her own, and she was trying to challenge this influence so my sister could reflect on her choice and make up her own mind. Either that, or she didn't relish having to cook a separate vegetarian dish every night! Whatever the reason, my sister's experience of group think was challenged, and when Elaine was not there to influence her she was exposed to alternative views and made up her own mind.

If this happened today, neither my sister nor Elaine would have needed to miss an instant of this battle for identity; the two could have maintained constant contact throughout the evening, further strengthening my sister's resolve and nullifying my mother's influence. My sister could have texted her friends about it, live-tweeted the whole evening or uploaded photos of the dinners and her reaction to them to Facebook in order to secure more support for her cause. In the late '80s, my sisters were restricted to one phone call per evening, which had a time limit. Now, adolescent-to-adolescent contact is near constant and largely unmonitored. 24/7 access to friends is possible, so there is little or no sanctuary from it. This is part of the always-on culture, which is worsened by the inability of young people to regulate themselves or the situation. I wonder if my sister would bow to the same peer pressure today, as it could be sustained indefinitely by smartphone.

The selfie, recognition and validation

The 'selfie' – a photo of yourself taken in order to post it online or send it to others – is a prime example of the relationship between technology and validation. These days, not only must written communication be instantaneous (responding to a text immediately, rather than waiting until you aren't mid-conversation with a friend) but *everything* must be captured and shared as it happens. This speaks to our need to be seen, to be validated. The selfie is a contemporary way of seeking and securing recognition, allowing us to be validated by the feedback we receive. Research also suggests that this need to share may be the result of narcissism or loneliness. There is also another kind of editorial work at play with selfies: we can manage others' impressions of ourselves.

The obvious concern about the 'capture it and share it' culture is that we run the risk of missing the moment in our attempts to capture and share it. I was at a concert recently where a very famous artist was playing one of his most iconic songs. While I was savouring the unique experience of one of my favourite artists performing one of my favourite songs, I couldn't help being distracted by a few of the people standing around me. The man standing next to me was recording the performance on his phone. On my drive home, I thought about this man and realised that he had been standing looking at this epic artist perform an iconic song through the screen on his phone. Surely the idea of watching the performance through a four-inch screen defeated the purpose of being there to see it live. It must have been more important to this man, and to the many others doing the same thing, to capture the event than to feel the experience first-hand.

It seems we have become more concerned with showing

we were there than actually being there. A great illustration of this change in recent years is a split image that made the rounds, composed of a shot of President Barack Obama's first inauguration alongside a similar shot at his second inauguration. The contrasted images show the crowd the first time clearly watching the ceremony and listening to what is being said, whereas the second image shows tens of thousands of smartphones held aloft above the crowd as they all attempt to capture an image to share.

The share

The adolescent clients I see refer constantly to the importance of the 'share', be it sharing a status update on Facebook, a tweet, an image or a music video. The most impressive aspect of the social media they use is its capacity to share so instantaneously and widely. The psychologist Aaron Balick writes in his book *The Psychodynamics of Social Networking* that the allure of the share is the recognition acquired through feedback in the form of 'likes', 'comments' and indeed further 'shares' or 'retweets'. Herein lies the power of the share: the sharer hopes that their funny tweet or an impressive image of them doing something exciting will generate a swell of positive feedback, giving them the recognition and validation of their peers.

However, we must consider the long-term impact of this kind of validation over time. Just who are these 'peers'? Just how nourishing to our self-worth should this feedback really be? In such a system, like my concert-goer watching the performance through his phone, having a new or important life experience – or any experience at all – is not the goal. The goal is sharing that experience and quantifying the positive feedback received by sharing. The value of the experience is being measured by external validation, rather than by the person who experienced it. The risk is that our judgement of our experience is formed not by our own set of values but by those of our 'friends' on social media.

This behaviour leaves us in a situation where the tail is wagging the dog in terms of how we experience emotions. Previously, if I had just been jilted by my girlfriend I would feel sad, so I might phone my friend to talk about it. I would have reached out to someone I actually know in real life, someone whose opinion I value, and asked for help. Sherry Turkle suggests that we have now moved away from this position of 'I have a feeling, so I think I will share it'. Today it is common not to know how to feel; instead, the impulse runs more along the lines of 'I need a feeling and so I will share.' Such an impulse may stem from boredom or a lack of fulfilment. The hope is that the feedback received will create feelings in the sharer, hopefully positive ones, and that the current moment that is devoid of a feeling will be filled. In interacting with social media in this way, we continue to merge technology with emotion and meaning in our lives.

The sociologist Irving Goffman ... suggests that we find out who we are through interactions with and reactions from others in our lives.

The sociologist Irving Goffman writes a lot about the formation of identity, the importance of feedback and managing others' impressions of ourselves. He suggests that we find out who we are through interactions with and reactions from others in our lives. Adolescence is the most pivotal moment in this process of identity formation; we can all recall trying on new identities as we progressed through our teenage years. There is photographic evidence of my own experiments with clothes, hairstyles and musical fandom throughout my teenage years that I still cringe to see, but such experimentation is entirely normal and developmentally necessary. However, our reliance on feedback during this vulnerable time is desperately important, and always has been, to adolescents. In times of uncertainty, like adolescence, we rely more heavily on the feedback and opinions of others to condone or condemn our choices; it serves as a sounding board to validate our choices about what type of adult we want to become.

The difference today is one of scale: vulnerable, hyper-sensitive teenagers are now trying on new identities and experimenting in front of 1,000-plus Facebook friends. This is problematic, particularly as feedback via a simple 'thumbs up' (or down) can lack empathy and be excessive in its tone and articulation. This validation and recognition that Aaron Balick describes as so central to identity formation is a potential minefield of mixed feedback online and can be overwhelming.

Some companies have cottoned on to this vulnerability and keenness for feedback and have set up specialist 'feedback websites', one of the biggest being Ask.fm. Here, young people are encouraged to give and receive feedback anonymously about all sorts of topics. This is a recipe for disaster: a large number of unsupervised, unregulated adolescents being actively encouraged to work out any issues that they may have with their peers, their parents or the world, without being identified. Anonymous anger and frustration can get displaced onto unsuspecting vulnerable adolescents who are looking for recognition and validation, but who can instead be subjected to torrents of abuse. This formula is always going to be far more likely to produce negative commentary than positive. In my clinical work I come across many young people who have been significantly adversely affected by these types of feedback websites.

Social snacking: the empty calories of 'checking in'

Keeping on top of all the different forms of communication across multiple social networking sites, not to mention the selfies, shares and texts, means checking in with them consistently. The consistent use of social networking and computer-mediated communication can be compared to snacking: you dip in and out, interact as and when you like and do so compulsively, without thinking, just like eating crisps. This is facilitated by easy-to-use, integrated social networking apps on smartphones that notify you when something happens on any of your social networks, and of course there's plentiful access to Wifi almost everywhere. Like eating junk food, access is cheap and everywhere, and practically impossible to regulate, and people (including adults) do it all the time. If we look at young people's engagement with their virtual community as social snacking, we can better understand its strengths and weaknesses.

Social networking activities such as posting, liking and commenting make for a quick, easy boost, a sugary rush of social energy from person to person – it's the junk food of communication. I describe it as such not to denigrate it but to get you to view it as an *extra* source of communication, a treat. Checking in regularly on our smartphone is fine, but it's not where we should be doing the bulk of our communication; the nature of its limitations means that the richness and meaning of a look, a warm embrace or even an empathetic conversation – the meat and potatoes of our communication diet – isn't there.

However, that is not to say that social snacking is all bad either. As I am known to tell my clients with eating disorders, there is no such thing as 'good' or 'bad' foods – there are only good and bad *amounts* of food. So if social networking or computer-mediated communication is like junk food, then we have to make a point to engage healthily with it. We know that most junk foods are fine in moderation and make for a nice occasional treat in addition to a stable balanced diet, but – and this is the crucial bit – junk food should not supplement or replace a balanced diet. Virtual relationships are similar in terms of their psychological 'nourishment': they are harmless once we have the capacity to regulate them. Children who grow up on stable and balanced diets tend to see snacks and sweets as an indulgence that they are treated to occasionally. Although they may desire junk food regularly and request it more often than other foods, they know how to relate to treats in a reasonable way.

Like many things, much of a child's relationship with food is mediated and regulated by their parents, whose most important role is to help guide their children towards making sensible and informed choices. Where this does not occur, and there can be many reasons for this, children may grow up on a regular diet of fast food, which they may grow to see as 'the norm'. The absence of parental role modelling and the ready availability of unhealthy alternatives mean that these young people are shown how to manage their diets poorly, possibly to a harmful extent. The virtual dietary culture is no different. We as parents need to show our children that we enjoy and value a balanced diet of face-to-face communication most of the time. So if we are answering emails at the family dinner table during a meal or tweeting while we push our child on the swing in the park, we're doing the technological equivalent of eating crisps for breakfast in front of our children.

THE WRONG SIDE OF THE TRACKS IN INTERNET CITY

Regulation of the internet

Regulating our children's use of the internet and helping them have the cop on to handle the constant barrage of feedback it provides them with will help them to navigate their way through Internet City successfully. As Stephen Fry points out, like any city, the internet has its fair share of nasty characters walking the streets and seedy neighbourhoods dotted around its more pedestrian areas.

One of the greatest challenges of the internet and online communication is that they are poorly regulated themselves. Many of the problems of online interactions are no different from those that have gone on since time began, but the internet operates on an infinitely bigger scale and in a more public – or entirely public – arena. Interestingly, many websites give great credence to self-regulation – usually through token gestures such as 'Do not click here if you are under 18 years of age'. This demands an unrealistic level of responsibility – and, again, of cop on – of intrigued and under-regulated adolescents who may well click through regardless.

The combination of behaviourally under-regulated young people, under-regulated internet access and the internet itself being an under-regulated and hugely powerful, potentially public tool for disseminating information instantly far and wide is a worrying one, to say the least. When we look at some of the more troubling aspects of internet use by young people, we can see just how important it is for our children to use their good sense to avoid trouble online and to ask for help when they need it.

Cyberbullying

The 24/7 element of online access has meant that bullying has taken on a whole new dimension. Bullying has been around for as long as any of us can remember, but there is a different quality to this act when it's online. 'Cyberbullying' was unheard of when I began working in child and adolescent mental health services, but now it seems to be everywhere in both the media and everyday conversation. Bullying of any kind is a big problem in child and adolescent mental health services, and speaking anecdotally I would say that bullying or being a victim of bullying is present in over 85 per cent of the children and adolescents I see. More traditional forms of bullying like name-calling, exclusion and threats of physical harm account for some of these cases, but many extend to online communication as well.

First off, I prefer to speak in terms of bullying behaviour, as opposed to labelling a child a 'bully'; labelling only serves to construct an identity for this young person, which, in the absence of an alternative, may be the identity they choose to live out. I define 'bullying' as persistent, negative behaviour towards another person, behaviour which is known to be causing them distress. The persistence despite the knowledge of the behaviour's impact is an important defining factor for me; a bully knows that their behaviour is upsetting their victim, yet still continues. Sometimes, a child can unwittingly bully someone, such as when a child who is aggressive and a child who is overly sensitive come into contact. The aggressor's banter could be labelled as bullying, when in fact the aggressor is not aware of the impact their actions are having on the other child. Naturally, if the behaviour is pointed out but persists it is most definitely 'bullying behaviour'.

In the past, like peer pressure, bullying or intimidation was limited to the school yard or the school bus, but when children came home and closed the door behind them, they were afforded a number of hours of peace from the torment ... Now, that period of sanctuary is gone.

In the past, like peer pressure, bullying or intimidation was limited to the school yard or the school bus, but when children came home and closed the door behind them, they were afforded a number of hours of peace from the torment. Children could use this time with their families to regenerate their self-worth or receive some positive feedback, which may in some way have stood them in better stead for the following day. Now, that period of sanctuary is gone. The bully can now reach you at home, while you're eating dinner with your family or doing your homework and even when you're supposed to be sleeping. This relentlessness is a considerable factor in disarming children's resilience in coping with such abuse.

We have invited this intrusion into our homes. Let's think about the progress that communication devices have made over the years. Before my time, there was typically one phone in a town or village, which meant that all the neighbours would travel to this place to receive important calls. Then we had the luxury of having one per house, but, if you recall, the phone was generally situated in the hall, away from the dinner table and away from the places where the family gathered. We then got a second or third phone, which was normally situated in our parents' room or the kitchen. Crucially, none of these situations was fully private, so parents could in theory regulate the amount of time spent on the phone, or at least be aware of who was on the other end and how often they were calling. We then moved to the cordless phone, which could be brought anywhere in the house but was still restricted to the house itself. Then came the mobile, which situated calls and texts in our hands. Finally the smartphone came with calls, texts, emails and the internet at our fingertips. This ease of access means that we can do any number of things from anywhere, but it also means that people we definitely don't want to hear from can reach us anywhere.

Sexualisation

Another concern that has developed during the technological revolution is the apparent escalation of sexualisation in children and adolescents. Some theorists contend that sexualisation has always been endemic in modern society and that Miley Cyrus's twerking is just the contemporary equivalent of Elvis's gyrating hips. There is a well-worn pattern of generational gaps when it comes to sexualised behaviours, but the generational gap this time around seems, again, more extreme.

There is nothing new in adolescent boys leering at glamour models in revealing dresses and the like, but modern-day children are bombarded with sexualised images in all sorts of contexts, from billboards advertising crisps to music videos. The sheer magnitude and constant nature of this exposure is the issue. Research shows that the many contemporary influences of sexualisation in adolescent behaviours include sexily posed, pouting profile pictures on social media sites to the daring themes involved in contemporary computer games. What is striking is how influential this can be, beginning with even very young children.

A 2012 study by Christine Starr and Gail Ferguson encapsulated the influence of sexualisation on younger children. Researchers showed images of two paper dolls to a large number of six-year-old girls; one was casually dressed and the other wore more sexually provocative clothes. They then asked the girls which doll they would rather be like. Almost 97 per cent picked the doll with the sexually suggestive clothing. The study also looked at what influenced children's views on or preferences for sexualised imagery and identified the usual suspects: the media, TV programmes and video games. However, what is encouraging is that the study showed that the number 1 influence on a daughter's views is her mother, so parents still have an important role in shaping the views of their children with regard to sexuality as they develop – and must manage this responsibility sensibly.

Learning about sexuality

When it comes to exposure to incidental sexualised images

and the likes of internet pornography, the issues of self-regulation and the inability of the internet to ascertain the age of its users are once again problematic, particularly when it comes to young people who are poor self-regulators but technologically savvy. My concern is what impact age-inappropriate access to sexual materials has on children who are only starting to develop their own sexual identity. Mental health professionals are increasingly concerned that online pornography may become the port of call for young people looking for baseline information about sex and sexuality, just as Google is now our source for everything we want to know. If Google sends a child researcher of the subject to a pornography site, which is quite likely, as there are far more pornography sites than sex-education sites online, then what they see there may set the bar for the information the child receives on what it means to have sex and be in an intimate relationship. According to social learning theory (the theory of how we learn through our social environment), a child in this situation will take away from the experience not what they see but the message implied by the images. So if they understand what they see on a pornography site to be a representation of an intimate relationship, then they will take this representation into the world as a fact – 'This is what an intimate relationship looks like' – which may have an impact on their behaviour, their attitude to and their expectations of intimate relationships. Adolescents are susceptible to being influenced in these sorts of ways in no small part because of their hormones.

We define many adolescent behaviours as the result of their infamous teenage 'hormones', yet how often do we discuss hormonal behaviour with our children? With the exception of that awkward 'birds and the bees' moment that lasts for five minutes but feels like five hours for everyone involved, when do we openly discuss sex and sexuality with teenagers? The reality is that we don't. It is therefore no wonder that they turn to the omnipresent Google for answers as to what is one of the most confusing and bewildering periods of their lives. As parents, we have to provide our developing hormonal adolescents with good, relevant sources of information – not a 25-year-old book with awkward illustrations or, worse, a direction to the ever unreliable Dr Google. I have learned from my conversations with young people that the sexual education curriculum in Irish schools falls short of what they feel they need and often does not provide a forum for questions. Involving an older sibling or an older cousin in the conversation is one way you can give young people an opportunity to discuss their concerns; you can also direct them to a reputable website with engaging and appropriate material.

Sexting

Another example of the interaction of contemporary technology and adolescent sexuality is 'sexting'. Sexting is the sending of text or picture messages that are sexual in content by mobile phone. Parents sometimes come to me because they have uncovered messages on their child's phone that contain sexual content. Naturally parents worry that their child may be promiscuous or sexually active and so bring them to therapy for treatment. Although I fully appreciate the concern, I do not agree that this behaviour necessarily merits psychological treatment, unless it is part of a broader psychological difficulty. More often, sexting or related online acts are the straightforward results of poor decision-making by the young person. Immaturity and a lack of interpersonal savvy, sense, sensibility and cop on are the issue. The good news is that children in these situations can definitively benefit from direction about these issues and develop more cop on in this regard.

Access to sexual material online

When I was deciding what group of people to use as my research sample for my doctoral research, I initially wanted to look at teenagers' social networking sites. But when I looked into it more closely, I came across some major issues that would have made my study unworkable. What I soon realised was that if I were to observe teenagers' social networking sites, I would possibly have ended up embroiled in a child-protection nightmare. Teenagers posting about their sexual adventures and misadventures is so common on these sites that, as a professional working with children, I would have been duty-bound to report so many posts for being 'inappropriate underage activity' that my study would have been unworkable. Undoubtedly, many of these posts are more bravado than reports of actual events, but it would still have been very difficult. It struck me that even the most mainstream social networking sites can be very sexualised environments for young people.

Though some of the research on young people's access to sexual material online is inconclusive, what we do know is that access to pornography at a young age is not a rare occurrence. A task force in the UK revealed some interesting statistics in 2012 in a government study of 14- to 17-year-old boys, of whom:

27% accessed pornography weekly
5% accessed pornography daily
58% had viewed pornography on mobile phones
40% had accidently clicked on a pop-up advert
25% received pornographic material in junk email
9% had been sent pornography by someone they know

The American movie industry produces around 400 mainstream movies per year, whereas the pornography industry makes around 11,000. The pioneering writer on pornography Linda Williams (2004) states that the pornography industry in the USA is not only bigger than the movie industry: it's bigger than its professional football, basketball and baseball industries combined. These statistics suggest that pornography is no longer the sideshow – it's the main event.

Online pornography in the home
Another eye-opening phenomenon that I come across with startling regularity in my work is young people discovering that their parents have been accessing pornography online, which makes them feel desperately uncomfortable. This occurs when a clumsy digital immigrant uses poor privacy settings, fails to search in 'private browsing' mode or doesn't clear their search or browser history. Whatever the reason, young people tell me about how finding out that their parents look at pornography significantly affects their relationship with them.

Generally, I tend to take a 'live and let live' view when it comes to the industry that produces legal pornographic material and to those adults who purchase or view it legally, but I cannot be dispassionate about young people being prematurely exposed to this material when they do not have the emotional or cognitive capacity to interpret it. Sometimes they are deeply affected by what they see. That this premature exposure happens as a result of parental negligence is even more problematic. Most parents are sensible and well adjusted, and if they choose to view online pornography that is indeed their right and their choice. However, when the children in their lives have access to these same laptops, tablets or mobiles, parents must be extremely careful that this unsuitable material does not find its way into their children's lives. Parents in this situation need to demonstrate their own cop on and must be extremely mindful of their children's access to their 'private material'. Many young people find that processing this kind of sexual material is just too much for them. We cannot 'unsee' what we have seen, so perhaps the consequences of these experiences will only emerge in time.

Young people need to have developed a degree of self-worth so that sexualisation does not become a central point of their validation. They already see that, in contemporary culture, good looks and sexuality are key to popularity and success and therefore they may feel pressure to appear to be more sexually mature – or, more worryingly, more sexually available – than they are. If we ensure our children understand that they have value and that they are worthwhile contributors to the world, they will feel less vulnerable and may not feel the need to do 'anything' sexually symbolic to fit in with their peers, online or off.

The digital line: the long-term effects of immature online activity

Regardless of where they go in Internet City, our children must be aware of the 'digital line'. This refers to the notion that, once information has crossed the line into the online world, it often cannot be got back. Even if we attempt to delete a post or an image from a device or social networking profile, it is often not really 'gone'. There is a good chance this data or image is saved on a server somewhere for some technologically savvy person to discover it. There's also the very real possibility that a post or image has already been captured, shared or downloaded by someone else.

There are long-term consequences to what we all do online, and once this digital line is crossed it cannot be uncrossed. In running internet-safety groups with young people, my colleagues and I have found that, just as children struggle to understand the long-term consequences of their actions offline, the same is true online. They have no awareness of the digital line, or when they might be crossing it. More mature and sensible young people know you should 'pause before you post', and consider the consequences of clicking a link, liking a post or uploading a photo. They take a moment and act with a degree of cop on, which prevents them doing something foolish or getting involved in something potentially troublesome. In order to encourage this kind of cop on, we warn young people that Microsoft statistics indicate that 47 per cent of employment offers are rescinded on the basis of information the potential employer found online about the candidate. This is but one example of how we must be aware that information we reveal about ourselves online is permanent and can be found by almost anyone, meaning that it may well have serious consequences for us in the future.

So is the answer then that young people should not have an online presence at all? Apparently not, because many people have been offered jobs on the basis of their online presence. A positive online identity can be very helpful in important areas like securing employment, beginning a romantic relationship and attracting friendships. It is the nature of our online identities that decides whether they will bring crisis or opportunity to us in the future. A young person made a very good point during one of our groups, declaring that the presidential election of 2030 will be very interesting: 'Nobody will be without dirt', he said. Somewhere, there will be photos that could destroy nearly every candidate. He cited the Irish presidential election of 2012, in which one candidate's bid for election was taken down by a tweet and an envelope, and he said he shuddered to think what the consequences of an online presence will be for candidates years from now.

Taking such a long and copped-on view is extremely rare in the young people I meet. No matter how much scaremongering adults try to do, young people often interpret limits on their online behaviour merely as attempts to control their freedom, not educating them about the risks involved. Helping our children to develop self-esteem, resilience and sense will allow them to make better decisions, both online and off. Over-protecting our children only further disables them from being able to respond when temptation inevitably strikes. Prohibition merely serves to drive the activity underground and ends communication on the subject between children and their parents. If we trust that our children have good sense, we can and should give them more freedom to negotiate all of these different challenges with cop on.

WEB 2.0: THE HUMANISATION OF TECHNOLOGY

If cop on regarding our use of the internet is important now, just think how much more important it is going to be as technology continues to evolve. Major companies and developers around the world work around the clock to devise technologies that serve us better; they want to sell technology that suits our existing needs more, and serves more of our needs, with a more personal touch. As technology becomes more personalised to us, it is often more humanised – which means technologies are purposely blurring the lines between what is real and what is not.

In her book *Alone Together*, Sherry Turkle describes trials of robots that are to be used in nursing homes for providing emotional care to residents. These robots, which often take the very life-like forms of animals such as seals, are programmed to imitate empathy by appearing to listen and even nod sympathetically as an older person talks to them. Technology is attempting to fool people with false empathy, thus pretending that it cares. A robot in a nursing home may well be programmed to respond in all the right ways and may play the role of a caregiver well, but, as Turkle points out, it is only an imitation. As a digital immigrant, I am immediately struck by these failings; I am critical of it because I developed my own sense of empathy and my understanding of the world in a very different culture. You may fob off this sad account as merely an extreme example, but, if you take a moment to think about it, there are many more subtle forms of this humanisation of technology in every Irish home.

The term 'Web 2.0' describes the increasingly interactive world of online technologies. This interactivity – the humanisation of technology – is believed to be the next step in information technology, and it's already here. The SiRi programme on Apple iPhone products is voice-activated software that allows you to 'interact' with your phone by asking it questions aloud. SiRi then 'speaks' and attempts to provide you with the answers. This provides an illusion that technology has a presence – SiRi is 'there' with you – and encourages you to interact with that presence. The more interactive and pseudo-human technology becomes, the more it will have an impact on how we relate to each other.

Most of us of any age are well aware that SiRi is not even remotely human, but the way that we speak about these assistive technologies can be telling. Take a sat-nav, which many of us have now in our cars or on our phones. The sat-nav 'talks' to us – in whatever accent we prefer; it refers to us directly and it tells us what to do. We consider whether we 'trust' our sat-nav, and we often refer to it by the gender that we have selected for the programmed interactive voice. A friend of mine told me that he was driving to a family wedding and had an elderly aunt as a passenger. He programmed the destination of the church into his sat-nav, and it duly gave him directions. His aunt commented, in all seriousness, 'Isn't she great, the way she knows the way to go?'

Interactive voice-activated devices have this effect on people of all ages, including digital natives. The talking toy is not new, but the sophistication of these technologies has evolved considerably in recent years. Where once there were Tiny Tears dolls that cried randomly or tiny on-screen Tamagotchi pets, interactive toys today make them seem prehistoric. Recently, my daughter received a teddy bear as a gift that came with details for logging on to a website. When I went to the website, I was asked to enter my daughter's name. The website then sent the information to the Wifi-enabled teddy, so that when I pressed the teddy bear's foot he said, 'Goodnight, Layla, let's listen to ten minutes of your favourite bedtime music,' before playing a playlist of music I had selected on the website. As far as my two-year-old daughter is aware, mostly because she is a digital native whose toys increasingly behave this way and because she does not have the cognitive capacity to understand the complexity of the programming element, her teddy bear knows who she is. After all, he calls her by name, he plays her favourite music and he responds to her.

One of the saddest things I have witnessed along these lines was a gift my first son was given, a very popular talking book. My sister kindly bought it for him as an early Christmas present, as he was very fond of the story of 'The Night Before Christmas'. But this was a talking book with a difference: it was designed to record my voice as I read each page, so that when I was not around or not available my son could open the book and press a button and my voice would begin reading the story for him as he turned the pages. It allows parents to 'be there' without actually being there. Certainly there is some value in this, if a parent is working overseas, for example, but by and large this technology fills me with sadness. It represents to me a tragic misconception of what story time for little children is all about; it's less about the story and more about the connection formed in those precious last moments of the day between a child and their parent. Story time at night is about the cuddles, the hugs, the interaction between you and your child and that warmth that can only be created in that moment between these two special people in a very special relationship.

If, for whatever reason, a parent is absent, using such technologies makes a degree of sense. But it doesn't take much to see how it could become a time-saving device. What if my son has to press a button to hear my voice because I see story time as ten minutes I can use to answer emails in the kitchen? We must as parents be aware of the technological power of persuasion that these 'advances' can bring and recognise how their use can change our real relationships with our children.

When we programme our personalities and needs into technology, we also allow technology to programme us. This is something to consider as technology grows and evolves into more and more aspects of our family and home lives. Digital natives may not recognise the extent of the power that their handsets and tablets have over their lives and how they live them, or just how lost they might become when they're transported to the sprawling expanses of Internet City. It is essential we teach digital natives the cop on to regulate how this evolution affects them, as their adult world will be even more technologically integrated and dependent than ours is today.

Section Three

COP ON IN ACTION: maintaining good sense in real life

B y now, I have established the basics of what cop on is, why it's important and how today's busy and always-online world can threaten its development in our children.

Now I'd like to complete the circle by looking at the different parts of cop on in more detail. If we understand the connections between our children's emotions, thoughts and behaviours, we can help them to work on their self-esteem. With that under their belts, they will be able to maintain a good level of cop on in their lives. I'll focus here on raising resilient children, giving them a sense of perspective and helping them to make good decisions.

Throughout this section, I will refer back to the technological examples from the previous section to put the elements of cop on in context, so that you can take away some food for thought, some practical examples and some real-life tips you can use to raise copped-on children.

———

In most parenting books, the 'how to' part tends to be the section of most interest to readers but that's not how this book is structured. Instead, I have written this book in sections that highlight the contemporary challenges that families and young people face and some of the possible pitfalls that may arise. Most importantly, I've shown the ways that you can help establish an understanding of your child in order to create a relationship in which you can successfully put some of the suggestions here to work. Like the metaphor of the jar of stones, which I'll explain below, you often have to put these ideas into action in a particular order, so it's essential that you develop the containing relationship as the foundation for any interventions. Once a healthy and open parent-child relationship is established using the advice from section one, and an understanding of the challenges of our on-demand world is achieved starting with the information in section two, then the 'how to' bits in section three can take place.

> *Once a healthy and open parent-child relationship is established using the advice from section one, and an understanding of the challenges of our on-demand world is achieved starting with the information in section two, then the 'how to' bits in section three can take place.*

So you've worked hard to develop and create a healthy relationship with your child, but you need to keep up the good work. How can you tell how your child's well-being and sense of self-worth are doing? Looking at their thoughts, feelings and behaviours is a good start. Next, try to find out their own view of themselves and explore their own critiques of their value and performance, their sense of their place in the world, their ability to be compassionate to themselves and others, and what value they place on external sources of validation. Establishing how your child reacts to the pressures and challenges of their world and what effect this has on their self-worth will reveal a lot and is worth doing regardless of how they appear on the outside. Even the most high-achieving children can experience crises of self-esteem, as we all do at one time or another. Comparisons with peers or siblings, a vulnerability to media pressures and an internalised need to achieve are things to look out for. If you do have reason to think that your child is a little harsh on themselves, then try to explore what this might be about.

BEHAVIOUR, THOUGHT AND EMOTION

There are behavioural, cognitive and emotional dimensions to all of us. Different schools of thought value each of these dimensions to different degrees. In trying to answer some of life's biggest questions, such as what makes us who we are, we should consider philosophical statements like 'I feel therefore I am', 'I think therefore I am' or 'I do therefore I am.' In my opinion, the best approach is 'I think, I feel and I do, therefore I am.' We are all made up of emotion (feeling), cognition (thinking) and behaviour (doing). Each dimension varies in its importance at different stages of our lives and from person to person. Understanding the dominant dimension at work in our children at any given time will better help us to relate to them.

Behaviour

In early childhood, our emotional and behavioural dimensions are at the foreground. That's because at a young age we haven't yet developed a sophisticated degree of cognition. Failing to recognise this when we're trying to relate to a small child can lead to communication problems. Simply put, this is why you can't negotiate with a toddler, as it involves a degree of cognitive complexity that the toddler has simply not yet developed. It is foolish to think that you can 'reason' with a toddler, because they are predominantly behavioural and emotional beings with little or no cognitive control over each of those faculties.

The majority of approaches for dealing with younger children are behaviour-based, such as a 'star chart', a reward system commonly used to modify small children's behaviour either at home or in the classroom. This simple concept involves rewarding positive behaviour and not reinforcing negative behaviour: good behaviour gets a star on the chart, bad behaviour does not. This premise can be really useful in engaging toddlers in behavioural change, and a modified version of the star chart is something I often recommend to parents.

The problem with focusing on behaviour alone in this way, however, is that it omits the emotional dimension. This is why, even when using a behaviour-based system like a star chart, it is important to recognise that some behavioural problems may stem from an emotional dimension. Anxiety is often expressed by whatever means are available to children at the time, so a more sensitive approach may be needed to see through the behaviour to the core anxiety. If your child is struggling to potty-train, then a star chart may be useful if it is accompanied with efforts to support your child's anxiety, such as reading one of the many fun, attractive children's books on potty training, which may help do away with some of the mystery of a new, intimidating activity. Children's fears or anxieties about doing something new that they don't understand often leads to bad behaviour, so it's worth stepping back and asking yourself what may be going on behind the tantrums.

Similarly, older children may act out at certain turning points because they are struggling to deal with new situations. This often occurs at puberty, when children are exploring what their sexuality means and may struggle to weigh what they learn at school, from friends and online against what they might want for themselves. Another typical time is the transition to secondary school, when the increasing complexity of emotional life of the teenage years becomes a feature. This is a monumental milestone for most children as they leave the 'spoon-fed' atmosphere of primary school for the hustle and bustle of a secondary school with a far more independent ethos. This shift in gear is considerable and many children struggle with this transition. If there are any underlying vulnerabilities that have been enabled or managed in primary school, these can become intensified and much more obvious in secondary school. It is in this transition that one of the first tests of resilience is often put in motion. The move to secondary school demands a level of grit, robustness, cop on and maturity in order for them to negotiate and survive unscathed. If a child lacks any of these qualities they tend to struggle with this adjustment, so try to be sensitive in your dealings with your child as they go through these kinds of changes.

Separation anxiety

The process whereby children individuate from their parents is essential to developing their resilience. Individuation involves a child separating from their parents – becoming their own person – at a pace that supports their level of autonomy and encourages them to learn new skills. The timing of the individuation process is crucial in terms of children's skill development and early development of robustness, resilience and cop on. This separation is an emotional process as much as a physical one; it involves children acquiring emotional coping skills as well as motor and practical skills.

The psychoanalyst Bruno Bettelheim has an interesting theory about childhood separation anxieties and fairy tales. Bettelheim suggests the reason that certain fairy tales have survived the test of time more than others is that they followed a particular formula. He hypothesises that the reason the great fairy tales, like 'Cinderella', 'Hansel and Gretel', 'Snow White' and 'Sleeping Beauty', are so successful is that they don't feature parents. Bettelheim feels that children take from these tales the idea that even the meekest can survive in the face of the ultimate loss, i.e. of their parents; that children can stand on their own two feet. He thinks children want these stories to be read over and over as a way to come to terms with the idea that their parents wouldn't be – and needn't be – around every minute of the day; they take solace in the survival stories of these characters. Perhaps J. K. Rowling tapped this same formula for her *Harry Potter* books in order to benefit from the universality of its appeal, for these long-standing stories address the truly universal process of individuation and the experience of separation anxiety.

Keeping the universality of this phase of development in mind, let us look at infant separation anxiety; the root of the emotional distress and challenging behaviour during this phase comes from children's intense fear that they will be abandoned. As this is both an emotional and a behavioural situation, you need an approach that will cover both dimensions. When children present with separation anxieties, they visibly 'make strange' or become distressed when separated from their parents or caregivers. When an older child (say five to eight years old) presents with separation anxieties, it often manifests as demanding behaviour, which their parents don't tolerate and punish. But children in this situation won't benefit from punishment; they need to be taught to be more robust and resilient by learning how to be alone, which can yield far more positive results. This can be done by a gradual weaning of a child's dependence on their parents by rewarding their capacity to be in a different room for short periods and reassuring them of their ability to cope in their parents' absence. A move away from endless attempts to 'reason' and 'negotiate' with your child instead concentrates on nurturing your child, and providing practical guidance and support to them in entertaining themselves will reduce your child's anxiety – not to mention your own anxiety about leaving your child alone. This adds a whole new dimension to the relationship and is a far more effective way of developing new skills in your child.

So, in short, emotions are what we feel (anxiety, sadness, anger, happiness, excitement and pride), cognition is what we think (I am in danger, I must be useless, I am going to be okay, I can do this) and behaviours are what we do (crying, not sleeping, being clingy, being violent; or being capable, assured, enthusiastic and composed).

Thought

The first thing that comes to our attention in the case of people of all ages is their behaviour, because behaviour is how we openly relate to the outside world. But behaviour is often the 'symptom' of the emotional or cognitive state. When we delve a little deeper, we often discover that certain behavioural changes mean that there are emotional and cognitive changes at work too. Red-flag behaviours that can indicate an underlying cause include drops in school grades, fatigue, changes in eating patterns, a loss of enjoyment in activities, social isolation, extreme sensitivity to rejection or failure, tearfulness, anger and irritability. Positive behaviours include an obvious enjoyment of activities, a network of healthy friendships and sociability.

Crucially, we must not overlook the power of our children's online world in shaping their thinking, be it by group think or a search for validation on social media or through pernicious cyberbullying. If, as parents, our own online worlds are not quite as pivotal to how we think, we must make a point to remember it is very different for our children; their mobile phones are a portal to a very influential world at a very important time in the development of their thinking and their mental health.

Cognitive changes mark a shift in how we think about our world. The red flags with regard to cognition include being overly worried, having ruminating thoughts, feeling worthless, having low self-esteem, feeling guilty, having difficulty concentrating and focusing on morbid ideas about life. Positive cognition includes a proportionate evaluation of your own abilities, an ability to enjoy activities for the fun of it and a positive sense of your worth and value as a person.

How we think about our world shapes how we experience it, so cognition plays a significant role in how we cope. This often comes down to the way we think about events and the type of lens through which we see the world. I will explore this further later in this section.

Emotion

Our behaviour and what we are thinking can be indicators of our underlying emotions, which are typically the most difficult to detect but also the most important. Our emotions are at our core, driving cognition, which then drives our behaviour.

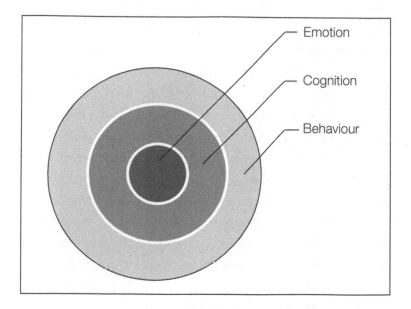

As parents, once we observe our children's behaviour, it is useful to work inwards to try to establish how they think about what's happening in their lives. This should reveal their belief and value systems and crucially how they value themselves, which is key to understanding your child. Our children's emotional lives can be difficult to get to grips with, but developing an open relationship with them means they will be more willing to talk about their thoughts, views, values, beliefs and feelings.

You may be wondering what this has got to do with resilience, robustness, cop on and self-esteem – and the answer is everything. We are all driven by emotion.

You may be wondering what this has got to do with resilience, robustness, cop on and self-esteem – and the answer is everything. We are all driven by emotion. It dictates our thoughts and our behaviours. Much of our developmental trajectory is dedicated to learning how to manage our emotion, which is the most difficult aspect of ourselves to control, as it is the most involuntary of our dimensions.

For children, emotionality is at the forefront of their being. This is true throughout childhood, but it is believed to peak during children's formative years and adolescence. There is no perfect way of managing emotion; we all know being too emotional or too unemotional is not helpful. So the ultimate goal of our emotional lives should be to find a way to negotiate our emotions effectively in different situations. This does not mean tamping down our emotions, as if emotions themselves were bad – far from it.

Developing emotional health in children

Awareness is important when it comes to emotion. Developing appropriate emotional responses requires awareness, whether the emotions are positive or negative. Call it nature or nurture – children tend to develop similar emotionality to their parents, and so it falls heavily on parents to guide their children's emotional development. Small children find it difficult to regulate their emotional responses to life events, but if they are made aware of what feelings are and are taught different ways to experience emotion, then they will learn how best to manage their emotions. If they are not encouraged to become aware of their emotional worlds, then their feelings will be supressed and their emotions will come to the surface through their behaviour.

*Small children find it difficult to regulate their emotional
responses to life events, but if they are made aware of what
feelings are and are taught different ways to experience
emotion, then they will learn how best to manage their
emotions.*

Working on developing your child's emotional intelligence
should not be confined to periods of upset or anxiety.
Teaching your child to be aware of their own feelings can also
help them understand how their actions impact on others.
As your child learns and grows, you can begin to get them to
be aware of more complex emotions like empathy, concern,
anger and sadness. This early development of an emotional
dialogue is crucial if your child is to bring emotional issues
to you in the future. I am amazed by the number of young
people who claim that they can't talk to their parents because
they don't 'do' feelings.

In light of the contemporary challenges caused by the
rise in social-networking sites and computer-mediated
communication and by the reduced time that parents get to
spend with their children, this emotional development has
never been more important. In a world which demands that
we confine what we have to say to 147 characters and reduces
emotional language to a series of emojis at the end of a texted
sentence, we must be on our guard against our children
becoming emotionally illiterate and unable to deal with
intense emotional states. Children are turning to chatrooms
instead of their families for help because they either do not
have the capacity to articulate their feelings aloud or feel that
their parents lack the capacity or the time to listen.

In a world which demands that we confine what we have to say to 147 characters and reduces emotional language to a series of emojis at the end of a texted sentence, we must be on our guard against our children becoming emotionally illiterate and unable to deal with intense emotional states.

Parents need to be mindful of keeping emotional conversations alive in order to ensure that their children become emotionally aware and emotionally honest. These two skills are cornerstones of cop on. They allow young people to experience an emotion, understand it, respond to it appropriately and seek help if they need it. With cop on, they are able to prioritise and contextualise emotion – the bedrock of good decision-making and cop on.

Children are turning to chatrooms instead of their families for help because they either do not have the capacity to articulate their feelings aloud or feel that their parents lack the capacity or the time to listen.

When you're worried about your children's emotions, thoughts or behaviours

'If it were your child, what would you do?' As I'm so often asked this by parents, in writing this book I had to ask myself what I wanted most for my children. My experience of treating young people with mental health problems and working with their families has given me some insight into the elements of the child-parent and parent-child relationship. Fundamentally, I think one of the most important things children should develop is the ability to communicate with their parents. This ability gives freedom and licence and the capacity for both parent and child to voice their worries and know that they will be heard.

'A problem shared is a problem halved' might be an overstatement, but I do agree with the sentiment that telling someone our problems definitely doubles the number of people trying to solve them. After all, I dedicate my working life to psychotherapy, which is built upon the premise of the 'talking cure', so it is in keeping with this belief system that I feel talking is valuable. The person you talk to doesn't necessarily have to have the answer; their presence and empathy can be enough in and of itself.

No matter what age your child is, showing them you are emotionally available – interested and ready to talk to them about their feelings, thoughts and behaviours – will mean a great deal to them. Some children are more willing to be open than others, but they all need to know that you're there for them.

> *'A problem shared is a problem halved' might be an overstatement, but I do agree with the sentiment that telling someone our problems definitely doubles the number of people trying to solve them.*

Loneliness

One of the most troublesome feelings we experience is loneliness, particularly if we are trying to deal with a difficult problem at the same time. Just as a problem shared is a problem halved, I believe a problem kept to yourself is a problem doubled. Secrecy or isolation often means that the original difficulty takes on a whole new series of different meanings and even more significance. Guilt, disgust and shame are frequently added into the mix if we continue to be alone with a problem, feeling that we are the only person who has ever faced such a challenge. In most cases this is untrue, but if we don't discuss it with someone else this myth of uniqueness can be all-consuming.

As adults we have the life experience and skills to understand that there is every probability someone else in the world has experienced problems similar to ours. However, children and adolescents may not be able to see this, as, for example, with teenage heartache when a relationship breaks up. In the immediate aftermath of a break-up, many young people become concerned that they are preoccupied with the relationship and spend hours ruminating over it; they listen to certain love songs over and over again; and they consider all kinds of ways they might get the person to take them back. Young people experiencing all these emotions often feel that they are 'going mad', that they're acting 'like a freak' and that, if they were to share their uncomfortable emotions, everyone would think they were crazy. When they eventually manage to convey all this to me during a therapy session, I am able to help contextualise and reframe their experience: it's called 'heartbreak'. Their thoughts, feelings and behaviours are not unknown to millions of others, including myself, who have experienced similar break-ups. I am always struck by how relieved and surprised young people are to hear this. The very idea that they are not the only person to have gone through this, and that others have survived, is a massive reassurance to love-sick teenagers. The power of someone connecting with us on a personal level and identifying with our experiences should not be underestimated in terms of the hope it can offer.

Often, love-sick teenagers say they 'wish they had mentioned it sooner'. They are delighted that what appears to be the most unique of challenges is not dissimilar to the experiences of someone else, and, even if the event is in some ways different, the reaction can be very much the same. That we have to share our problems before we can get the benefits of engagement and support from a trusted relationship is a core lesson that young people need to learn, and I worry that these days the skill of sharing our problems is becoming lost. With all our computer-mediated communication, the art of articulating a feeling out loud and in person seems almost alien to young people, but it's a skill we as parents must ensure they bring with them into adulthood.

Why do young people keep it to themselves?

One of my core aims for myself as a parent is to be approachable. In order to establish this, we must be aware of the barriers that stand in our way. In my experience, young people decide not approach a parent out of a fear of a number of reactions. Children fear that they will be judged, get into trouble or cause anger, upset or disappointment in their parents. They worry that confiding in their parents will result in an excessive response which will cause them further difficulties or in a privilege they value being taken away in order to prevent further problems, such as online access or their mobile phone, for example. These anticipated responses are often not the actual responses their parents have when an experience is eventually disclosed, but children's fear is an undeniable reality, and so they often remain secretive.

To prevent your child from keeping their difficulties a secret and trying to manage them alone – something that can happen even at a very young age – you need to communicate to your child that they can tell you anything at all, and ensure that they know your response is going to be helpful. This can be incredibly difficult to do in practice, as we are all human and we all get angry and upset or are disappointed by what our children say. Nonetheless we have to manage our responses to our children's problems so that lines of communication and support stay open.

LEARNING TO HAVE GOOD SELF-ESTEEM

Good self-esteem is crucial to being able to manage your emotions, thoughts and behaviours and is a central part of cop on. Although our personal temperament is a determining factor in self-esteem, we can all learn to improve our self-esteem and to improve our children's self-esteem. Creating a household that encourages lasting personal values like honesty, kindness, friendliness and being a good person will certainly cultivate a child's self-esteem within that family home. Self-esteem involves valuing the many different facets of ourselves and recognising the value in our more enduring qualities. Therefore we must try to promote these values in the family home, and recognise and reward our children for valuing these qualities in themselves and others.

The Irish inferiority complex: a cultural disposition

Some cultures struggle more with the concept of self-esteem than others, and, as a rule, the Irish don't encourage it. It is often frowned upon to show a liking for yourself, and it can be seen as being arrogant or smug. When I tell young people that it's important to like yourself, many squirm in their chair just thinking about it. We have a collective notion that to love yourself is somehow wrong or unnatural; loving yourself is a point of view that is often mocked. Bill Cullen, the successful Irish businessman and TV show presenter of 'The Apprentice', is a great example of this. Mr Cullen is a guest on many TV and radio shows and often speaks about how, when he wakes up in the morning, he stands in front of the mirror, pumps his chest out and tells himself, 'Go, Bill, you're the greatest, you can do it.' He reports using this strategy as a way of developing a strong belief in himself and the self-confidence he needs to take into the business world and use to his advantage. As a public figure, he has received a great deal of criticism in the media for this attitude and has become an object of ridicule in some satirical radio shows. For the Irish, doing these sorts of self-confidence-building exercises is an alien concept. Irish culture seems to only value excessive humility; sometimes I feel that we as a people associate honour with self-denigration.

With this in mind, when I talk to young people learning to love themselves, I have made a point over recent years of changing my terminology. I no longer talk about self-esteem or self-love, but instead refer to having 'self compassion' for yourself, which seems more palatable to an Irish audience. The difference is small, but the effect of changing the focus from 'loving yourself' to 'giving yourself a break' has had a noticeably positive effect in terms of young people's willingness to buy in to the concept. If we promote a culture of compassion for ourselves among our children, we will teach them how to relate compassionately to themselves in times of perceived failure; this will of course fuel their resilience and cop on. Indeed, an understanding of compassion on a personal level will help them to treat others with kindness and understanding – and a bit of cop on – as well.

Distinguishing self-esteem from self-confidence

Self-confidence is how we project ourselves outwards into the world. It is how we 'carry ourselves'. Self-esteem is more about our internal world – our relationship with ourselves. Self-esteem is a more nurturing and sustaining feature than self-confidence.

Let me explain. Firstly, self-confidence is not necessarily a recipe for happiness. Someone can have high levels of self-confidence but low levels of self-esteem. For example, when I give lectures to young people in schools, I illustrate this point by saying that I am confident I can deliver the content of the lecture – I know I can stand up in front of a room full of transition-year students and talk to them about mental health. I can do this because I am confident in my knowledge of mental health as a subject. I know it, I have studied it and I am able to deliver a talk on it. However, that is not to say that when I get into my car on my way home I won't evaluate my performance negatively. I might think that I was rubbish, the talk was useless and the students thought I was no good. My self-confidence allows me to get up and do the talk, yet my self-esteem leaves me feeling lousy once the talk is over. Self-esteem can therefore be more powerful in terms of how we experience events and it can even inform our future self-worth.

Good self-esteem or spoiled brat?

I was asked recently to do a talk in Dublin for parents for which the organiser asked me to focus on self-esteem. In her opening address, she said that she wanted children in her school to know what it was to find the line between liking themselves and becoming 'arrogant, tyrannical spoiled brats'. This is the challenge for parents: if we 'big up' our child's ability too much, will they have *too much* self-esteem? How do we get the balance right?

The tail that wags the dog

Good self-esteem is *not* thinking you're the bee's knees. It's not about having an over-inflated sense of self or being over-confident. Self-confidence is how we project ourselves to the rest of the world; self-esteem is how we relate to and evaluate ourselves. It is possible to possess a lot of confidence but to have very little self-esteem. One of the main challenges to our self-worth and self-esteem is that we overvalue a single, typically negative, aspect of our lives, which can turn into a 'tail wagging the dog' situation. Common examples of this include thoughts like 'If I were thin, then I'd be happy' or 'If I were popular, then I'd be happy'. In actual fact, if someone were genuinely happy, then they would not 'need' any of these things, and if we did gain happiness by becoming thinner or more popular, we would probably only strive to be thinner and more popular still. To prevent the tail from wagging the dog, we must develop a stronger sense of our multi-faceted nature and establish the difference between wanting to do well and needing to do well. Children with good self-esteem may want to do better to add to their already robust sense of self; if they have good self-esteem, they will have the resilience, grit and cop on to handle it if it does not happen. When children need to be the best, they may struggle to adjust to a perceived failure. 'Need' means that this accomplishment defines their self-worth, whereas 'want' means it merely adds to their other accomplishments.

A multi-faceted view of children today

In addition to the Therapeutic Milieu model I explored in section one, there are a few other ways you can help your child become a well-rounded individual. One is to adopt a rounded and balanced view of the world. If they have such a view, children will have a good degree of self-awareness and will be able to regulate their responses to events in line with their developmental level. They will also value themselves and their experiences to a healthy degree.

Such an approach has many layers and is necessarily nuanced, and it can be really difficult to hold on to such a 'messy' view when we live in a world in which we're encouraged to think that the latest smartphone, Facebook like, retweet or Snapchat selfie will make us happy. The more vulnerable among us, who are desperate for happiness, may be seduced by this idea of instant happiness and believe in its myth. In order to challenge such influences, it is really important to help our children develop a more balanced view of the world and a more comprehensive view of themselves.

If our children are taught to see themselves as people with multiple positive and negative attributes, they will be able to draw upon the stronger parts of themselves to counteract any problems they may be having in another area of their lives. Knowing they can do this will make our children more resilient: it is so important that they *know* that they have the ability to overcome difficulties. Teaching our children that we have many qualities of different but equal value creates a metaphorical toolbox of skills they can use to manage different situations. If, for example, your child does not do well in a test, or they get let down by their friends, or indeed they are being bullied, it is vital that they do not let these isolated experiences become measures of their worth. A child who has been taught that they are multi-faceted and have different positive qualities will have the cop on to realise that a single disappointing experience does not define them, so they will recover from it.

Parents spend a lot of time telling their child that they are good at lots of things, but that is not necessarily a recipe for good self-esteem and self-worth. A constant stream of positive reinforcement doesn't teach a child *which* of their good qualities are more important, nor does it correct qualities that need improvement. What's more, some children may interpret compliments on their achievements as pressure to achieve even more.

Consider instead that some of your child's qualities are more valuable and more meaningful than others: honesty, kindness, friendliness and compassion are far more sustainable elements of who they are than, say, their appearance, performance or online persona, and should be recognised if you want them to grow. These qualities will grow in accordance with the emphasis you put on them, so the old adage of 'catching your child being good' is especially relevant here. It reminds parents to praise their children when they are doing something well, rather than leaving well enough alone. It stems from the principle that the visibility and recognition, concepts I defined in section one, serve to encourage further good behaviours. So if, for example, you have two children who normally fight with each other and one day you notice them playing quietly together, the understandable temptation may be to leave them at it.

Instead, you should make a point to say how nice it is to see them playing together and possibly reward them with an unexpected treat. Try to be as passionate about commending good behaviours as you are about tackling difficult ones. If you reinforce your children's good qualities, you will show them that you value those aspects of their personality and want to see more of them.

> *Be as passionate about commending good behaviours as you are about tackling difficult ones.*

Two types of jigsaw-makers

Sometimes I meet young people who have a tendency to focus on what they don't have – be it material goods, physical attributes, online friends or anything else – and ignore what they do have. To these young people I often tell the tale of the jigsaw-makers: 'There are two types of jigsaw-makers in the world. When they reach the half-way point in making their jigsaws, they have two different reactions. The first sits back, looks at the half-finished jigsaw and says, "Gosh, haven't I done well! I can see the picture forming and it looks good. I am nearly there." The second sits back, looks into the box and says, "Oh, my God, look at all these pieces I have left to do. How will I ever get this finished? This is going to take for ever!"' We all have to decide which kind of jigsaw-maker we are. Are we content with being that jigsaw-maker? If not, we have to decide to change.

The jar of stones

A story I often tell about a jar of stones illustrates perfectly the effect of we how prioritise the important things in our lives.

This story was allegedly first told by a philosophy professor, who entered a full lecture hall holding a large glass jar and a collection of bags containing different types of stones. He filled the jar up to the top with the biggest rocks. 'Hands up,' he said to the class, 'if you think this jar is full.' The majority of the class held up their hands; after all, the rocks went right up to the top of the jar. The professor then proceeded to take out a bag of smaller stones and pebbles and shook them into the same jar. The pebbles fell into the cracks between the rocks and tumbled down through them. He shook these in until they reached right to the top of the jar. He then asked the class, 'Who thinks it's full now?' Again, most of the students raised their hands. The final bag he opened was full of sand, which he poured into the jar. The tiny grains of sand found space in the cracks between the rocks and pebbles and trickled all the way down to the bottom, filling the jar to the top. He again asked the class to raise their hands if they think it's full. The majority of the class stuck up their hands.

The professor then explained the metaphor behind this exercise. The large rocks represent our primary relationships, like family and close friends. These are the relationships in our lives that are most meaningful and give us a sense of ourselves. The pebbles represent important things like our job satisfaction, academic performance and monetary earnings. The sand represents everything else, like our popularity online, awards or material possessions. But the significance of this exercise was only revealed when he explained to the class that the important thing is not how full the jar is, but in what order you fill it. If you fill the jar with the rocks first, the pebbles second and the sand third, you'll get the greatest variety of objects into the jar. But if you start with the sand, the jar will fill right away and there will be no room for the pebbles or the rocks. Likewise, if you fill the jar with pebbles, there will only be enough room for sand – none for rocks.

What this wonderful visual exercise shows is that if we overvalue the less important or more materialistic forms of validation in our lives, there will be no room for our more meaningful close relationships. It is something of a vicious circle, for without these formative relationships we risk prioritising less important aspects of our lives over the more sustaining and nurturing aspects. The idea behind this jar of stones exercise is to understand that our value systems are only truly meaningful when we base them on a meaningful context. This is an essential component of cop on and good decision-making. When children truly understand the value of their relationships, they see the true importance of all the different dimensions of their lives and become better decision-makers.

The show reel of my life

This capacity to step back and see things in context has been an important learning curve in my own life. As challenges arise from time to time, I have had to learn how to take a breath and see the bigger picture. Recently, I was due to give a lecture at UCD, and, despite leaving myself an hour and a half to get there, I was going to be late. The traffic that morning was horrendous; I remember being stuck at a traffic light in Dundrum for ten minutes without moving. I began panicking about the 190 students sitting in the main lecture hall waiting for me. I then realised I was thumping the steering wheel as the lights turned green and then red as no one moved an inch. I was irate. But then I took a moment and considered what I was really feeling. In fact, my anger was more an expression of my high levels of anxiety than it was about the traffic. I began fantasising that I was never going to be asked back to give a lecture in UCD again after being late for this one. I tried frantically to phone the organiser of the lecture to inform them of my delay but the signal was engaged. At one point I gazed out into the car next to me and saw two small children, who were mesmerised by my visible distress. They had clearly seen me looking furious only moments earlier and were frightened. I had a moment of clarity and decided to cop on to myself. I put my arms on the steering wheel, took a couple of deep breaths and asked myself aloud, 'Does my happiness depend on this moment?'

After a few minutes of rationalisation, I realised that it didn't. I imagined being an old man lying on my deathbed and realised that when the show reel of my life began to play, neither this traffic jam nor any fallout from my being late would feature at all. That show reel would remind me of my great friendships, my experiences of falling in love, my graduations, the births of my children and the magical moments we shared. It would not, of course, feature a rainy Tuesday stuck in gridlocked traffic in Dundrum. By doing this short exercise I was able to find some context for my experience and I was able to gain a perspective that wasn't riddled with anxiety, so I calmed down. In short, I copped on, and since then I have kept up the habit of taking a breath, counting to ten and asking myself if my happiness really depends on this moment. It introduces a sense of context where it's lacking, and I feel it has helped me greatly.

Challenging unhelpful thinking styles

One of the most common self-esteem busters is unhelpful thinking. These are the 'automatic negative thoughts' we all have at some time. This kind of thinking actively damages our self-esteem, resilience and self-worth. It can spread quickly among peer groups through social networks in real life, but even more so online, where extreme behaviours and commentaries tend to attract the most attention. Some of these unhelpful thinking styles can become habits over time, so I am going to outline some of the ideas of the cognitive behavioural therapist Aaron Beck here to help you identify them in yourself and your children and to show you how best to manage them.

Generalising

Making sweeping judgements based on limited experience is something we all do at times, and it's particularly easy for children to fall into this habit, as their experience of life is necessarily limited. Consider a child training to do the long jump. She is aiming to do a 'personal best' jump but doesn't make it on her first attempt. She thinks, 'I'll never be able to jump that far', and gives up without trying again. She is now, of course, correct: she will never be able to do it if she doesn't jump again. The net result of this thinking style is that it prohibits her from continuing to practise and improve. The key to challenging this unhelpful thinking style is to encourage the child to have some grit and stick at it. She needs to stand back and realise that, just because it doesn't work first time, it doesn't mean she won't be able to do it at all. This attitude also helps encourage the child to enjoy the fun of being on the team and going to practice for its own sake. Having a more positive attitude to the experience as a whole might even improve her end result.

Selective thinking

Selective thinking causes people to concentrate only on the bad parts of their experiences and pay no heed to the good parts. If young people decide they hate school, when they think about school they will only think about the subjects they dislike. They won't consider their friendships and the social side of school, which they might really enjoy. As a parent, your role is to provide perspective to your child and get them to see any troublesome experiences in context in order to challenge this one-dimensional perspective.

Complete disaster thinking

A tendency to catastrophise leads people to presume not only that they will fail but that everything they do will be a complete disaster. Take a child who has to make a model for his art class in school. In the process of making it, he finds that one part of his model is not exactly how he'd like it to be. Because his model isn't perfect, he proceeds to tear up the entire thing and put it in the bin, losing all perspective of the significance of one flaw in a much larger project. The role of the parent here is to try to manage the child's expectations of himself. No one is equally good at doing everything, so imperfections are inevitable. Learning to cope with minor errors and to distinguish them from major problems is part of life. Challenging this all-or-nothing perspective is important if the child is to learn how to be resilient in the face of future disappointments.

Challenging your own negative thinking styles

Children and anxious young people are not the only ones who engage in unhelpful thinking styles; you will no doubt have recognised yourself or another adult you know in the examples above. We all have a tendency to do it from time to time. Because it's so widespread, being a good role model to your children is even more important when it comes to challenging their unhelpful thinking styles. Self-esteem is about being good enough and accepting who you are, warts and all. As a parent, you provide the blueprint for your child of what is an acceptable perspective to take in the face of life's challenges, so think what sort of message you're sending when you say things like 'I'm really rubbish at that' or 'I'm so stupid sometimes'; your child will learn from you and think that it's acceptable to think about themselves that way too.

Letting the scene set the soundtrack

It is imperative that as parents we show our children how to have a healthy way of looking at the world, because they are impressionable and they can lack the experience to reconsider an off-kilter view of the world. For example, the child of an anxious parent may sense a potential threat in everything. Unlike an anxious adult, though, the child's cognitive abilities aren't well enough developed to manage that anxiety or weed out real from imagined threats to their well-being.

The lens through which we see the world can colour our whole experience, which was once superbly explained to me by a young person I met. Rather than using a visual analogy like a lens, he thought of it more as a 'soundtrack to a scene'. A camera can be set up to capture any scene, let's say a coastal landscape, but it's the accompanying music that usually sets the tone for the scene – say, in this case, the song 'Oh, What a Beautiful Morning'. If you take exactly the same scene and play the famous music from *Jaws* in the background, the scene changes meaning completely. So, as parents, we should allow the scene to dictate the soundtrack, and not the other way around, to ensure that we and our children have a healthy and flexible approach to reacting to what the world throws at us.

RAISING RESILIENT CHILDREN

Flexibility and a positive attitude are important to being resilient, but resilience isn't purely reactionary. In addition to aiding us in reacting well to whatever life sends our way, resilience also demands that we be true to who we are. We must have enough cop on to be able to prioritise one experience over another based on its value *to us* – regardless of what everyone else thinks. This is particularly important when it comes to our online lives, where what everyone else thinks spills onto our screens in a constant stream of status updates, shares and tweets. If children do not develop a strong ability to prioritise, they might value things that are trivial, passing and materialistic over other more important aspects of their lives.

Take, for example, a teenager who is disappointed by getting poor scores in his summer exams. He seems down about it; it is hard for parents to know what to do to help him, but this is a good opportunity to try to teach him about the multi-faceted aspects of his personality, abilities and experiences. He needs to see that his academic ability is just one aspect of who he is; after all, in the grand scheme of things, his summer exam results are not as important as he thinks they are. He has other qualities that are far more enduring and important than his ability do well in his summer exams.

To take another example, if this book doesn't sell well I will have to make sense of that experience. I may well be upset about it; I imagine I may even take to my room and cry about it. However, I would hope that, over time, I'd be able to make sense of the real impact of the situation. In time, I should be able to say, 'Look, my book didn't sell. There could be a hundred different reasons for that. Does that make me a bad person, or a failure? No, it does not. There is plenty of evidence to suggest that I am good at many things. I'm a good dad and my children like me. I'm a good son and my parents often appreciate that. I'm a good therapist and people often thank me for my help. I'm a good friend, who thankfully is surrounded by many people I care about and who in turn care about me. So, in summary, does the fact that my book did not sell define who I am as a person? No, of course it doesn't. I need to dust myself off and get on with my life, and either chalk my authoring days up to a "lesson learned" or learn how to write better-selling books.'

Resilience and protecting our children
Given all the contemporary challenges I have discussed, it is important to realise that it is simply not possible to protect our children from all eventualities. The internet, technology, drugs, alcohol, unsavoury friendships and relationships, pornography, early sexualisation and risky experimentation are all part of growing up in contemporary western society. It is not a case of 'if' your child will come across these aspects

of life in Ireland today but 'when'. The fantasy for all parents is to be able to protect their children from these experiences and to sterilise their environment, but this would prevent their children from learning to cope with these challenges. As children mature and individuate from their parents, it becomes increasingly difficult for parents to maintain the kind of environment they were able to provide when their children were infants and toddlers. Going to school automatically exposes children to many new experiences, so they need to be prepared and supported so that they'll be able to respond to them. A child who is over-protected may be unable to cope with or manage challenging situations in their lives. Some parents take this advice to mean that they need to make their child 'tough', but I will clarify below why this is not the case.

Who wants a tough child?

It's worth pointing out that when I speak of a child who is 'resilient' and 'robust', I am referring to an emotional strength – not physical or interpersonal strength. No one wants their child to be the meek and vulnerable child in the group, but nor do they want their child to be the playground brute. What's more, a socially domineering child is not necessarily the most resilient child, because being tough on others can be more of a sign of a lack of resilience than an abundance of it.

To my mind, a copped-on child is one who achieves the right balance between being caring and pleasant and being able to stand on their own two feet and be true to who they are. Using this definition, you couldn't describe a playground bully as having a lot of cop on.

Getting a sense of perspective

It is not the event but the reaction to the event that matters

Imagine a situation in which ten people share a similar experience of a trauma. For the sake of illustration, let's imagine they are involved in a hostage situation and are held captive in a bank during a robbery for hours until the police arrest the thieves, and the hostages are released, physically unharmed. Five out of the ten people are heard saying things along the lines of 'Oh, my God, I nearly died. You know what? Life is too short. I am going to seize the day from now on and make every day count. I am going to climb Everest and go on that holiday I have been dreaming about, and I am going to ask that woman I have fancied for years out for a date.' These five survivors respond to the trauma by embracing life and now feel that their days need to be enjoyed to the full. The other five survivors of the exact same incident say, 'Oh, my God, that was awful. I nearly died. My life could have been over! The world is a dangerous place and I don't feel safe. I am going under my duvet and never coming out.' They do not view the experience as a 'near miss'; instead they focus on the negative and frightening aspects of the experience.

These two responses are manifestations of the different levels of resilience, self-esteem and coping skills among both groups, as all of these things help to shape our responses to adverse events. That is why we need to prioritise resilience and cop on as important life skills for our children, especially as these days it is so easy for young people to be influenced by the constant barrage of their peers' opinions, moods and takes on shared situations as posted and shared online.

Resilience is something that is learned over time and picked up by children over the course of their development.

We are all products of our own experiences, so how we interpret our experiences will either make us stronger and enable us or weaken our resolve and disable us. Like many of the true qualities that stand to us throughout our lives, resilience and cop on cannot be developed overnight, but they are qualities we can build into the fabric of our parenting by displaying and actively working on these skills ourselves and discussing them with our children. How a parent responds to disappointment, frustration and failure will help their child learn skills of resilience, so it is essential they have a good role model in you. As parents, we need to manage and hone our skills of resilience, such as expectation management, calmness and good prioritisation.

The psychotherapist Isabel Menzies Lyth famously said, 'It is better to contain failure than to fail to contain.' This simple sentence encapsulates so much for me. What she means by this is that certainly failure will happen; we don't necessarily need to set about avoiding failure but to establish a system to manage it when it does happen. Menzies Lyth says it is our response to failure, rather than failure itself, that defines our true abilities. Resilience is central to responding well to failure and disappointment, as resilience is made up of an awareness of strong values and an ability to evaluate accurately the true value of things and experiences. This is only possible if we have a multi-faceted understanding of the qualities of the human subject. If we believe that having awards, trophies, medals, Bitcoins and hundreds of Facebook friends makes us more valuable as people, then we have a very one-dimensional understanding of the human subject. However, if we feel that valuing kindness, friendship, loyalty and understanding is important, then this will give us a broader, more meaningful context for failure if we do not achieve the goals we had set out to achieve.

Why expect the worst? That sucks!

Managing expectations lest things go wrong is an important thing for children to witness in order to learn. But chipping away at outlandish expectations can sometimes be taken too far if we teach them to expect the worst as a matter of course. In Ireland we tend to have a collective low self-esteem, and our expectations and hope can be disproportionately low, to the point where we seem to fear hoping for better or being seen to have too high hopes. It's a culturally pervasive philosophy that lives by the motto 'Expect the worst so whatever does happen is a bonus.' Although I can see the rationale behind this oft-quoted concept, as a philosophy it weakens our self-esteem by indicating that to have hope is simply a bad idea. Leaving Cert students awaiting their results often say that they feel their exams went well enough, but they're afraid to hope for better lest they be disappointed. By adopting the philosophy of assuming the worst, they may spend their whole summer after sixth year in a panic or feeling gloomy about their expected results. A bit of cop on here goes a long way towards striking a balance between expectations on either end of the scale. Copped-on young people are able to judge an event in the context of their own experience and have reasonable expectations for the event's outcome.

Expectation management is about realising that at some point you may fail but that you will be able to respond to it and cope; it is not about expecting to fail from the outset. I always tell young people that they will at some point more than likely fail a driving test, go for a job interview and not get the job, or indeed even fall in love with somebody who doesn't love them back. It is highly probable that life will throw many of these situations at them (and at everyone else), and, although these experiences will be difficult, they will be able to cope.

The value of 'meh'

One of my favourite words in the online Urban Dictionary is 'meh'. This very popular contemporary colloquialism brilliantly captures the sense of 'so what'. Using the term 'meh' can have a truly protective quality for the speaker when it comes to managing disappointment. For example, consider the following situation: Tina stands at her locker in school as she sorts out her books. She turns to say hello to Mary as she passes by. Mary says nothing. Tina becomes consumed with wondering why Mary didn't say hello. 'What's wrong with me?' she thinks. 'What did I do?' Tina becomes preoccupied and anxious that she has upset Mary in some way. Liam is standing at the lockers farther down the hall and has the same experience with Mary. He turns back to his locker, shrugs his shoulders and says, 'Meh.' This simple example shows how the child with low self-esteem and poor resilience scrutinises their every move and ruminates for long periods about the most benign incidents. You can see here how unhelpful thinking styles kick in, as Tina is left stressed and worried for the rest of the day.

The resilient child responds with the 'so what' mentality. Liam thinks, 'I don't know what's going on with Mary, but I'm not going to get hung up worrying about it,' and moves on with his day. The resilient child can contextualise the experience by assuming that their peer is having a bad day or even that they did not hear them. As we'd all likely admit, most of our updates on social media aren't worth a second thought either, so developing a sense of what really matters will help our children to sift the wheat from the chaff in their online worlds too. These internal context-forming dialogues create resilience in children and protect them from becoming overly absorbed in their interactions with others. Resilient children have good enough self-esteem to think, 'Screw them, their loss' or 'Who cares?' and have the cop on to decide that certain interactions aren't important enough to merit further thought. Resilience and self-esteem play a central role not only in managing anxiety but in good mental health more generally. These qualities allow young people to develop coping mechanisms and deflect or digest the inevitably negative experiences that will come their way.

Digging deep

It is during adverse life events that people tend to 'show their true colours' or 'find the strength from somewhere'. To me, this response to adverse events is true heroism at work.

In team sports, a true hero is the player who plays well when the team is under pressure. It easy to play your best and display your full array of skills when your team is well on top. After all, your coach and fellow players are feeling positive, your supporters are delighted and singing in the stands, and you are likely enjoying positive feedback instantly, whenever you make a good play. There's even often room for some show-boating when losing the game is not in question. But when the team is in trouble and a loss appears imminent, it is much harder to perform; you're stressed, your coach and fellow players are dispirited or panicking, your supporters have fallen silent with worry, and you might well receive negative feedback from them if you stumble or make a mistake. It's a recipe for disaster.

A number of years ago, while playing for Manchester United, the controversial footballer Roy Keane was involved in a Champions League semi-final against Juventus. During the game he received his second yellow card of the tournament. This meant that he was ineligible to play in the final if his team won the game. Sports commentators still talk about his performance after getting that second yellow card. Quite simply, he played the game of his life. He ran 'box to box', covering every blade of grass on the pitch and tackling furiously. What Keane was able to do was contextualise his own failure in getting two yellow cards and see the greater cause at stake, which was for his team to get to the final. Although ordinarily I would never claim to be a big fan of Roy Keane or his management of his other noteworthy footballing experiences, in this instance he displayed true grit, cop on and a bit of sporting heroism. The real measure of our ability to dig deep is when things are going against us.

Building our resources to help us get through tough times involves absorbing the many positive experiences in our lives and using this positivity and our knowledge of these experiences to gain perspective when things go wrong. Having the right perspective in troubled times can help to power us through anything from a minor upset to a major, life-changing negative event.

The Patronus Charm
There is a wonderful example of this concept of positive experiences being called upon to manage negative

experiences in the *Harry Potter* books. In the books, Harry is faced with mythical creatures called 'Dementors', who suck the happiness out of a person so they feel that they will never be happy again. Harry has to learn how to fight off these Dementors, which are basically a physical manifestation of depression. The method of conjuring the anti-Dementor spell (known as the 'Patronus Charm') is to focus on your happiest memory and then enact the spell. Interestingly, Harry struggles to find a truly happy memory, which shows just how hard it is to be positive or find positive things when we are feeling sad. Nevertheless, after practice, the spell works and has significant meaning for Harry, as it is connected to the love he received from his parents. The message inherent in J. K. Rowling's story is that it is in our early positive experiences that we have the beginnings of the reserves of positive experiences we can add to as we go through life. We can draw upon these reserves and gain strength from our past positive experiences in response to difficult life events.

MAKING GOOD DECISIONS

A child with cop on is one that successfully develops an internal mechanism for decision-making. This is far preferable to an over-reliance on external decision-making, as when parents curtail internet use for their children, which is often very difficult, if not impossible, to institute.

The purpose of this book is to look at ways in which we can build the internal mechanisms for decision-making and problem-solving that protect our children by fostering their resilience and coping skills. In my work I see many young people who make poor choices and poor decisions, which are sometimes made because of low self-esteem, unrealistically high expectations, a drive for the extraordinary or a poor sense of self. Encouraging our children to become good decision-makers is not simply about coaching them in how to respond to challenges, but about addressing any underlying issues they may have.

It makes sense that if children value themselves, they will then be able to make decisions that do right by them. This should mean they make decisions and choices that protect themselves rather than put themselves in danger. Likewise, having a degree of self-worth should mean they are less likely to make decisions that undermine their value. Conversely, children with low self-esteem can act out or behave in such a way that they are placed in potential danger. Also, if children have unrealistically high expectations of themselves, they often prioritise achievement over their own well-being, which can cause them to become overwhelmed with the stress of expectation or to act out in resistance to it, feeling that no matter how well they do or how hard they try they will not be good enough. Neither of these scenarios bodes well for developing a copped-on decision-maker.

> *I want children to be tempted and to know how to make the right decision when they are. I want them to make mistakes and to learn from these mistakes, and most of all I want them to understand their many qualities and to value what is meaningful in their lives.*

When my son is a teenager and finds himself with a group of his peers who are bored, they may decide by way of amusement to go to an old abandoned house in the area to break windows, drink cans of cider and generally get up to no good. Should this happen, I want him to think about the consequences of doing this and whether it is a good idea or not. My hope is that his own sense of resilience will come into play and he will decide not to go, despite what his friends may think. I then hope his cop on will come into play when he considers how to get out of going and help him come up with a plausible reason not to join them. I'd like him to use the same skills to avoid comparable problems 'on the wrong side of the tracks' online too.

Some might say I am being ridiculously naïve or that I want my child to become a goody-two-shoes. But being copped on is not about being a goody-two-shoes; it's about having a degree of savvy and an ability to think on your feet. This savvy will allow my son to protect his relationship with his peers and save face in the way that he cuts out before the trouble starts; more importantly, using his savvy, he will be able to make decisions that are based on good problem-solving and sound priorities. He may well come home disgruntled and irritable and be angry with me or his mother, feeling that he has missed out on going out with his friends, but I hope that over time my son will understand he has made the right decision, be comfortable in his own decision-making process and, ultimately, be happy with the end result.

Raising a critical consumer

Ideally, our children will be able to question the waves of influence that come their way with a healthy, questioning mind. As in the example above, children with cop on will be able to work out the best choices for them by examining the pros, cons and possible consequences of a situation and by making a value judgement based on these factors. Using their cop on in straightforward ways like this will also make them a critical consumer of the wider world in simple ways, such as when they make purchases online or in person. They will also be critical consumers in more complex situations – of information – questioning the true value of what they're told and what they read and of the websites they visit.

The importance of savvy

Being a critical consumer is only half the battle; it's equally important for young people (and all of us) to think critically about what they contribute through their attitudes and behaviours. Being savvy is something I feel young people at the moment often lack. Most teenagers don't realise that the more you tell your parents, the less they will ask. Understanding this takes a bit of cleverness, an ability to see the big picture and the capacity to think like someone more mature than yourself: your parents. It means having enough respect for your parents to be truthful with them, even if you find it irritating and invasive to have to 'check in' with your parents about what you do with your time. But it also means having enough respect for yourself to play the long game and to value your freedom enough in the long term to sacrifice it in the short term. The 16-year-old who tells his parents where he is going, who he will be with and what time he will be back generally gets let off without much interrogation. If he returns on time and without any drama, then he earns more trust and gains more freedom. By being savvy and responsible, he communicates to his parents that he's fine; he has cop on.

His sister, however, doesn't tell her parents where she's

going, refuses to say who she will be with and argues about the time she should be back at. In part because they don't have much information to go on and in part because she's being defensive, her parents are suspicious and want to keep an eye on her. She hasn't offered them much respect, and she clearly hasn't seen the big picture. Each curfew she misses means she will lose out on the leniency afforded to her brother, and so a long battle of will ensues, which will make it worse for her. She isn't being savvy and she certainly displays no cop on in this situation.

ALL THINGS IN MODERATION: AN EXERCISE IN COP ON

I've now explored many different facets of cop on and how it can help our children navigate our on-demand world. Though it's always worthwhile to consider the subject in depth, it's more important to be able to put this approach into action in simple, practical ways.

Some say that cop on is something you cannot teach. I disagree. I have come up with a simple but effective way of teaching our children the skills of cop on, and perhaps, of borrowing some of the tips for ourselves. This method boils down what I've explored throughout the book and should be the basic approach that you take away with you.

The 4–7 Principle

The beauty of this principle again lies in its simplicity. In order for us to teach our children to make good decisions and measure their reactions to life events, we must first introduce them to the concept of moderation. Much of the stuff of mental health problems is born of a lack of moderation. From food, alcohol and negative thoughts to hyperactivity, anxiety and obsessive or risk-taking behaviours, they all thrive on a lack of moderation. I believe that if we can moderate and regulate our behaviours and our thoughts we are less likely to run into trouble. This is why the 4–7 Principle is so important.

How to do it

Rate everything you do from 1 to 10: your work effort, alcohol intake, spending, anxiety, stress, sleep, food intake, exercise – everything. See how you get on across the board. Then look at the specifics. If you find that your rating in a certain area is low, in the 1–3 range, or high, in the 8–10 range, then try to address it. If you find that your anxiety is a 9, then work to pull it back into the 4–7 range. If your exercise rating is a 2, then bring it up to the 4–7 range. This will help to show you which areas of your life lack moderation, and it will give you a simple way to monitor your behaviour and to work to improve it. As you learn to self-regulate, your accomplishments will instil in you a measured response and a collectedness that will stand to you – as cop on.

You can also harness the power of technology in improving your own cop on. Personally, I put a reminder in my smartphone that repeats on the middle Wednesday of every month and simply reminds me to 'take stock'. When I get this message, I try to take five minutes out of my day to do exactly that. I take stock of my work life, my academic life and my family life. This simple process forces me to 'hold up the mirror' and brings to the forefront of my mind the things I need to be mindful of. This helps me to stay on task and gives me an opportunity to consider how I can exercise some of the suggestions that I am doling out to you, the readers of this book, and it might be useful to you as you work through some of the ideas here with your family.

CONCLUSION: ENOUGH COP ON

Over the course of this book I have highlighted the challenges of the world today and how recent societal changes influence the most fundamental aspects of who we are. Technological advances and cultural shifts have changed how we communicate, relate, respond and cope and what we expect, desire and demand. We can see the effects of these changes on how we relate to each other easily enough, but it is considerably harder to identify how these changes have altered how we relate to ourselves. Our understanding of who we are, what we are worth and what we need and deserve in turn affects our relationships with each other and with our families. As parents, we need to be alive to these influences, develop strong relationships with our children and try to teach them the traditional skills of coping that are at risk of being diluted by today's world.

Cop on allows us to read a situation for what it's really worth by putting it in a broader context and prioritising it to a reasonable degree. Cop on is about giving each situation the right amount of attention at the right time by reacting appropriately to events and remaining measured in our responses. If we use the Therapeutic Milieu model to nurture cop on in our children, we will be able to judge the right balance of each of its five elements and utilise them sensibly, as best suits each of our children. Cop on is about being contained, structured, supported, involved and validated *enough*.

For me, cop on is a marker of 'enough': enough self-worth to know your own value, to avoid selling yourself short when it comes to friendships and relationships and to know when you've done enough experimenting with risk-taking and testing boundaries. It's knowing when to say, 'Enough is enough', emotionally, so that you can work on relationships and experience feelings without becoming overwhelmed. Cop on means having and maintaining enough close, meaningful relationships in your real life to feel supported and enabled in striving for independence.

For me, cop on is a marker of 'enough': enough self-worth to know your own value, to avoid selling yourself short when it comes to friendships and relationships and to know when you've done enough experimenting with risk-taking and testing boundaries. It's knowing when to say, 'Enough is enough', emotionally, so that you can work on relationships and experience feelings without becoming overwhelmed. Cop on means having and maintaining enough close, meaningful relationships in your real life to feel supported and enabled in striving for independence.

The 'cop on' approach to raising children is about getting the balance right – the right amount of containment, support, structure and everything else this book takes on. Make no mistake: raising children with cop on requires a strong sense of parental cop on too. Cop on is a 'life skill' in the truest sense of the term: it's a skill developed in childhood that most certainly carries into our adult lives and it is central to our role as parents. As parents, we need to exercise a serious level of cop on in the face of so many challenges, but, with a bit of work and a bit of luck, our children will carry their cop on with them through life and maybe even inspire cop on in their own children some day.

In today's world we can become complacent when it comes to cop on. With all that there is to distract us and keep us busy, it is easy to get sidetracked and lose a sense of what is important. As parents, we need to make time to reflect on what we do to actively build our own cop on and encourage our children to do the same. Make a time for some sacred space or some screen-free time at home. This needn't be as extreme as it sounds; it turns out it is practised even by top IT developers in their own homes. A recent article in the *New York Times* looked at some of the biggest names in technology and their attitudes to allowing their own children's screen time, and what they found was really surprising. You may have imagined that in Steve Jobs's house there was an iPad in every room, but not so. Across the board, Jobs, his colleagues and their competitors limit their children's exposure to technology and are very strict about the amount of screen time that their children are allowed, if indeed they permit them to use technology at all. This must tell us something. If the very people who created these technologies see a need to limit their children's exposure to them, then surely there is a lesson in that for us. Make time to connect and relate and talk. We need to unplug from the online world at times and spend some uninterrupted time with our children and ourselves. Hold up the mirror for a moment and see if you don't catch yourself missing things or missing out – missing opportunities to spend face-to-face time with our children and missing opportunities to spend some time with ourselves.

In helping to stem the tide of fleeting values, omnipresent stress and online demands, our work towards giving our children a bit of cop on is perhaps only a small effort in the right direction. Yet if, with a bit of cop on of our own, we do manage to raise our children to be self-assured, resilient, independent young people, we will have done ourselves, our families and our society proud.

As digital immigrants, we see the trick behind the magic. It's like knowing how the magician creates the illusion. It alters fundamentally how we comprehend it. As digital natives, children cannot see the trick; they see only the magic, and therefore we need to understand that this is all they know, and it is an entirely different relationship.

Texts cited and further reading

Beck, Aaron T. (1972), *Depression: Causes and Treatment*. Philadelphia: University of Pennsylvania Press.

Bettelheim, B. (1976), *The Uses of Enchantment: The Meaning and Importance of Fairy Tales*. New York: Random House.

Bion, W. R. (1957), 'The differentiation of the psychotic from the non-psychotic personalities'. In E. Bott Spillius (ed.), *Melanie Klein Today: Developments in Theory and Practice. Volume 1: Mainly Theory*. 1988. London: Routledge.

Bion, W. R. (1959), 'Attacks on linking'. In E. Bott Spillius (ed.), *Melanie Klein Today: Developments in Theory and Practice. Volume 1: Mainly Theory*. 1988. London: Routledge.

Bion, W. R. (1962), 'A theory of thinking'. In E. Bott Spillius (ed.), *Melanie Klein Today: Developments in Theory and Practice. Volume 1: Mainly Theory*. 1988. London: Routledge.

Bion, W. R. (1962), *Learning from Experience*. London: Heinemann.

Bion, W. R. (1963), *Elements of Psychoanalysis*. London: Heinemann.

Bion, W. R. (1970), *Attention and Interpretation*. London: Tavistock.

Bion, W. R. (2005), *The Tavistock Seminars*. London: Karnac.

Borg, J. (2008), *Body Language*. London: Pearson.

Boyd, D. (2014), *It's Complicated: The Social Lives of Networked Teens*. New Haven, Conn.: Yale University Press.

Byrne, C., 'Generation tech: More kids can play computer games than ride a bike'. *Venture Beat* [online magazine] (19 January 2011), <http://venturebeat.com/2011/01/19/kids-technology/>.

Centre for Clinical Interventions (2008), *Back from the Bluez*, [information pack], <http://www.cci.health.wa.gov.au/resources/infopax.cfm?Info_ID=37>.

Children's Commissioner, *'Basically... porn is everywhere' – A Rapid Evidence Assessment on the Effects that Access and Exposure to Pornography has on Children and Young People* [press release] (24 May 2013), <http://www.childrenscommissioner.gov.uk/content/press_release/content_505>.

Chua, A. (2011), *Battle Hymn of the Tiger Mother*. New York: Penguin Books.

Cohen, C., 'FoMo: Do you have a Fear of Missing Out?'. *Daily Telegraph* [website] (16 May 2013), <http://www.telegraph.co.uk/women/womens-life/10061863/FoMo-Do-you-have-a-Fear-of-Missing-Out.html>.

Cross-Tab Marketing, 'Online reputation in a connected world' [market research report commissioned by Microsoft] (January 2010), <download.microsoft.com/download/c/c/2/CD233E13-A600-482F-9C97-545BB4AE93B1/DPD_Online%20Reputation%20Research_overview.pdf>, accessed November 2014.

Dunbar, R. I. M. (1993), 'Coevolution of neocortical size, group size and language in humans'. *Behavioral and Brain Sciences*, 16(4), 681–735.

Gunderson, J. (1978), 'Defining the therapeutic process in psychiatric milieus'. *Psychiatry: Journal for the Study of Interpersonal Process*, 41, 327–35. Cited in Pratt, C., Gill, K., Barrett, N. & Roberts, M. (2006), *Psychiatric Rehabilitation*, 2nd edn. New York: Elsevier Academic Press.

Headstrong (2012), *My World Survey: National Study of Youth Mental Health*. National Centre for Youth Mental Health, School of Psychology, University College, Dublin, <www.headstrong.ie/sites/default/files/My%20World%20Survey%202012%20Online.pdf>.

Lyth, I. M., 'Social systems as a defence against anxiety', *The Modern Times Workplace* [online network of resources], <http://www.moderntimesworkplace.com/archives/ericsess/sessvol1/Lythp439.opd.pdf>.

Mischel, Walter, Ebbesen, Ebbe B., and Raskoff Zeiss, Antonette (1972), 'Cognitive and attentional mechanisms in delay of gratification'. *Journal of Personality and Social Psychology*, 1(2), 204–18.

Mischel, W. (1966), 'Theory and research on the antecedents of self-imposed delay of reward'. In B. A. Maher, *Progress in Experimental Personality Research*. New York: Academic Press, 85–131.

O'Reilly, G. & Erkan, Y. (2011), The Pesky Gnats CBT App. Cork: DeCare Systems Ireland.

Prensky, M. (2001), 'Digital Natives, Digital Immigrants, Part 1'. *On the Horizon*, 9(5), October 2001, 1–6.

Rowling, J. K. (2004), *Harry Potter and the Prisoner of Azkaban*. London: Bloomsbury.

Ryan, S., '2,700 texts per person sent in Ireland', *thejournal.ie* [online newspaper] (May 2012), <http://www.thejournal.ie/eurostat-yearbook-survey-european-union-448928-May2012/>.

Sheldon, P. (2013), 'Voices that cannot be heard: Can shyness explain how we communicate on Facebook versus face-to-face?', *Computers in Human Behavior*, 29(4), 1402–7.

Skues, J. L., Williams, B., and Wise, L. (2012), 'The effects of personality traits, self-esteem, loneliness, and narcissism on Facebook use among university students'. *Computers in Human Behavior*, 28(6), 2414–19.

Starr, C. R. & Ferguson, G. M. (2012), 'Sexy dolls, sexy grade-schoolers? Media and maternal influences on young girls' self-actualisation'. *Sex Roles*, 67(7), 463–76.

Storlie, Jean, 'Jar of Stones'. Storlietelling [website] (7 August 2013). <http://www.storlietelling.com/2013/08/07/rocks-pebbles-sand-a-story-bite-about-the-important-things-in-life/>.

Turkle, S. (1995), 'Ghosts in the machine'. *Sciences*, 35(6), 36.

Turkle, S. (2004), 'How computers change the way we think'. *The Chronicle of Higher Education*, 50(21), 26.

Turkle, S. (2011), *Alone Together*. London: Karnac.

Twenge, J. M. & Foster, J. D. (2008), 'Mapping the scale of the narcissism epidemic: Increases in narcissism 2002–2007 within ethnic groups'. *Journal of Research in Personality*, 42(6), 1619–22.

Urban Dictionary [website], <http://www.urbandictionary.com/>.

Winnicott, D. W. (1960), 'Counter-transference'. In *The Maturational Process and the Facilitating Environment* (Ch 14). London: Karnac.

Winnicott, D. W. (1962), 'Ego integration in child development'. In *The Maturational Process and the Facilitating Environment* (Ch 4). London: Karnac.

Winnicott, D. W. (1962), 'A personal view of the Kleinian contribution'. In *The Maturational Process and the Facilitating Environment* (Ch 16). London: Karnac.

Winnicott, D. W. (1963), 'From dependence towards independence in the development of the individual'. In *The Maturational Process and the Facilitating Environment* (Ch 7). London: Karnac.

Winnicott, D. W. (1963), 'Communicating and not-communicating leading to a study of certain opposites'. In *The Maturational Process and the Facilitating Environment* (Ch 17). London: Karnac.

Winnicott, D. W. (1971), 'The use of an object and relating through identifications'. In *Playing and Reality*. Hove, Sussex: Brunner-Routledge.

Winnicott, D. W. (1971), 'Mirror role of mother and family in child development'. In *Playing and Reality*. Hove, Sussex: Brunner-Routledge.

Winnicott, D. W. (1971), 'The transitional objects and transitional phenomena'. In *Playing and Reality*. Hove, Sussex: Brunner-Routledge.

Williams, L. (2004), *Porn Studies*. Durham, NC: Duke University Press.